Lust…

to explore the

thoroughbred woman in you?

I dedicate this book to

all women in this world

Thanks to all of you for your being, acting and acting
the world presents itself so varied and colourful!

Book & Set design by Carmen C. Haselwanter
Translation by Bill Renieris

Carmen C. Haselwanter

Lust...
to explore the thoroughbred
woman in you?

You have everything in you!

Inside you there is a thoroughbred woman. Live as one!

Bibliographic information of the German National Library
The German National Library lists this publication
in the German National Bibliography; Detailed bibliographic data are available on
the Internet at http://dnb.d-nb.de.

ISBN: 978-3-907151-20-4
www.creativita.cc

Table of Contents

Foreword

Dear Readers

Thank you for pursuing your interest and wanting to know more about this topic. Thank you for grappling with this original theme of being a woman. It is a gift, a miracle. Women are a fascinating creature with a wealth of skills and talents that humankind has managed to bring to the present century. This would not have been possible without the women. Women are the centre of attention in many cultures without which the system would not work. In many circles, women work harder than men work, sleep less, and are constantly working. As mothers, they are constantly alert in their sleep, because of their children. Women are a marvel. In addition, women carry a variety of other versatile skills, which are covered by the many everyday tasks.

I am writing this book in the Du form. Why? By doing so, I directly address your soul. Compared to the she-form, which is rather impersonal, the du-form fits much better this topic.

Yes, I wrote this book for women, but that does not mean that this book excludes men as readers. On the contrary! Sincerely, I invite men to read this book. You will learn to understand the women better. By reading this book, men will embark on the wonderful journey of discovery of the female sex and will learn to love and appreciate the wonderful female attributes even more.

I do not know if you bought this book, because the title "Lust ... to explore the thoroughbred woman in you?" Immediately appealed to you and now you are curious and curious to read these lines. Alternatively, did you get this book for free? Maybe even from your partner? You were initially outraged when you read the title. Maybe you even wondered if your partner asked if he found you were not completely his wife? Are his children born of you more than proof of that?

However that book got in your lap, I beg you: see it as a sign! There is always a reason why certain information reaches a person. Everything has its purpose. I invite you to embark on this journey of discovery. You will experience wonderful things as soon as you let go of your doubts. Whereby it can quite happen that you disagree also with diverse writings, yes I like you even my words outrage. That may be. Remember that everything is your mirror. Words that touch you, whether positive or negative, let you look inside yourself. In it you will find answers. I will talk more about this phenomenon later. That may not be pleasant. Sometimes even very uncomfortable. However, this possibility offers you that you can take along a lot for you. Get involved in this experiment. What do you have to lose? You can only win.

If you do not like this book, I ask you to pass the book on. Everything has its resonance, its inevitable effect. Completely according to the law of cause and effect. Passing on knowledge has a nourishing effect that has a positive effect on you. Passing on knowledge and continuous learning, today we are equipped with this sensational technology.

Last but not least, I want to wholeheartedly ask you to make of your life a masterpiece. You are worth it! You have everything you need. You were given all the gifts in the cradle. Do not wait, but actively pick up your scepter and live the life you desire. You were born for that.

With these thoughts, wholeheartedly wish you the strength, energy and the consequence that you live your life according to your wishes and dreams. Live your thoroughbred wife thoroughly. Always remember that you carry the inheritance of Eve and Cleopatra in you. Live this with pride and dignity.

With these words, I wish you all the best and love!

Yours Carmen C. Haselwanter

Why is this book a must ?

Every year thousands of books are being written. Some of the books deal with issues that explain. The others touch people with their content. This book has the purpose of doing both. On the one hand to show you different perspectives & on the other hand to touch your heart.

Why should you as a woman read this book?

You are a woman and wonder why this book is a must? You as a woman know how women tick. How you tick yourself. Is that really so? Ask yourself deep in your heart, if this is really the case. Have not you often caught yourself several times asking yourself one or two questions and not knowing the answer? Did you even consult your best friend and did not go home wiser after hours of discussion?

Yes, you are a woman! I too am a woman and know very well that we women are often a big question mark to ourselves. Welcome to the club! So get involved in this journey here. Dare to take the step to learn more about this species of woman who has so many talents and talents. I would like to congratulate you too! First, that you read this book and venture the journey into the fantastic world, and that you are a woman! The wonder of nature has chosen you to be not a man, but a woman. A wonderful creature, a thoroughbred woman, with unbelievably many abilities, far above those of the male creature. I would really like to congratulate you on that dear companion.

Be proud that you carry the legacy of Cleopatra, who, as an invincible thoroughbred woman with her charm and deeds, brought several men to their knees and went down in history. As a descendant of this fascinated woman, you also carry her inheritance in you. An inheritance whose enormous power, love and energy can move mountains. Also from you!

Is this book as well something for men?

It is clear! I also wrote this book for the men's world. Because women are a myth for many men. An inexplicable entangled gender that actually means, "*yes*," even though it says "no." How should a man know about this? Men love women! For the moment, they usually love the female body and the imaginative joint activities that are brewed in their heads, which in all their colours and forms are transformed into wild sex. Well known.

What do women want? Deep down, women want men's appreciation, respect and, of course, monogamous love. They also want men to cherish, love, touch, respect and understand their mind, heart and, not least, their soul.
So honest ladies: Do not we ask too much about the men's world?
My dearest Men: This book is intended to help you to better understand the ladies' world. **Have fun exploring!**

What is the purpose of this book?

I want to encourage women with this book. Would like to inspire the ladies of this world to recognize their own ingenuity, greatness, uniqueness. I want to show what you are all about, what unbelievable abilities are in you, just waiting for them to be released. So that these skills can be unfolded in idleness.

Believe me, ladies! Every single one of you has enormous potential. Just see what each one of you does in a single day. The bulging daily necessities you do day after day again. For the benefit of your family, your children, your family! Question: What do you do for yourself? With this book, I want to urge you to raise your own dreams, your deeply buried desires from the sinking.

Remember, that there are still dreams you have buried.

Stop with the ostrich strategy!

We humans like to accept and accept situations as given. No matter how unintentional this is. In the so-called ostrich strategy, man tends to put his head (metaphorically) in the sand and thereby let everything pass over him. To accept abuses. Instead of questioning critically, perceiving options and counteracting accordingly, the ostrich strategy does exactly the opposite. This is now over! Now is the time to take a serious look at your essence to name things and take action. As a result, you evolve from an ostrich animal to an active panther, who takes his destiny into his own hands. Are you ready?

Who is behind the author name?

Born in Austria, my parents gave me a Spanish given name. My black hair and blue eyes perfectly matched that racy name. Not 6 months later, I was blond and had green eyes. It almost seemed as if my outward change was a tender hint and harbinger for my way of out-of-line dancing.

At the age of 17, I left home to do my first foreign experience in London. An exciting time began when I discovered my gift for communication and the urge to research. In addition, I found it intriguing to deal with people of all cultures, races, ages and backgrounds. The learning of each language was a challenge that I accepted with great enthusiasm. Since I left home in 1987, I live abroad. Inhabited tens of man countries and always dealt with people. I began to study people, listened to their stories inquisitively and learned with each word.

Learning and teaching is a passion I have been practicing for many years. Be this as a coach, entrepreneur, manager, artist, writer & photographer! Above all, as a woman who always follows the call of her soul!

Why did I write this book?

Since I can think, I am fascinated by people, especially women.
In doing so, I have repeatedly come across the phenomenon that women usually make the impossible possible without much attention and attention to their environment. Thanks to her grace, will, patience, strength and incredible energy. So I started writing my experiences and insights very early on the travels. It was already clear to me then that these texts in book form should find the way to

other people. I have written this book for all women in the world. It is a gift to the wonderful creature, which usually receives too little attention, respect & love. Recognizing & perceiving what women do in their everyday lives, putting them on the right track and putting themselves last is a bitter downer that does not do justice to women.

Does this book also serve as a gift?
Yes! True to the motto: *"The more people read this book, the more positive change it will effect"*. Making the world a better one starts by sharing knowledge. Giving away books is helpful. I love personal books and give them away very happily. I always have good quality and quantity of books in stock and, depending on the situation, I have a book handy to hand it over. What could be better than passing on knowledge? Whether this book is valuable as a present depends on the person. In my opinion, this book is suitable as a suitable gift for teenagers as well as for pensioners.

No one is too young or too old to learn. As soon as we leave the womb as a baby, learning is an indispensable part of our lives. Although society tends to discard this need as irrelevant to the older generation, it is even more important for older people to engage in learning on a daily basis. Because only those who learn daily stay awake and young in the mind and body.

So I can advise you to give this book away. It is not a 0815 book at all. It may also happen that the gifted person does not agree with certain sections of the book. Yes and? Do not let this come to you as a donor. You pass on knowledge. That is extremely commendable. I would like to congratulate you. Providing people the opportunity to change their perspective, and thereby broaden their perspectives, is a great honourable act. Knowledge makes life better, more colourful, wider and enormously expands the perspectives.

Knowledge is power.

Remember that only used knowledge changes. Goethe summed this with the sentence: *"It is not enough to know - you also have to apply it."*

Use what you read best

Every day we read numerous texts, emails and much more. At the same time, what is read is superficially perceived. I like to invite you to accept this book not just as a casual text. As a writer it is important to me that you take with you as much as possible. It is therefore recommended, that you use this book as a workbook, in which you write your thoughts, ideas and impressions directly.

What is the best way to handle this book?
>You hold an information & workbook in your hand. Therefore, invite yourself to actively use this. Face the questions and exercises. It is your very personal workbook, which only you work with!

>**Write down your thoughts, mark text passages,
>add your notes on the edge.**

>Use this work to get to know you again. It is the best way to get all the essence out by critiquing the questions, actively doing the exercises, and writing your answers directly into the book. In this form you get out the best inputs and benefits.

>Make sure that you do not read the book in one. Since this is a workbook, you should take the time to work through it in a timely manner. **This takes time. Take your time!**

Highlight in Action
>For this, it is ideal to have a pencil, eraser and highlighter at hand while working through each text passage and actively use. This will help you highlight important texts by using highlighter markers. The pencil is a great way to capture notes and thoughts from the edge while filling in the question passages with your answers.

>By adding your own thoughts and notes, you personalize this book

and make it your work. I wrote the book for you, just for you. So use it so that you can get the most out of yourself.

Seek out the most important statement.
In addition, it is helpful if you choose from the beginning of the two pages lying in front of you always your most important statement for you. By writing them down in the upper right-hand corner, you can make these findings visible to you at a glance.

Everybody feels touched and attracted by something else. You will see that the importance of the statements will change over time as well. This is perfectly normal and reflects the passage of time. What was important to you yesterday lost a lot of importance today. However, it is crucial that the then meaningful in your development supported you to your present being. In this respect, everything that appeals to you at a certain time has its importance. In this respect, give this sign your attention and meaning.

At the end of the chapter
Here I recommend that you collect the most important information, principles and insights for you and record them in writing at the end of each chapter. This helps you to crystallize the quintessence.

As soon as you reach the end of the book, write down all of your important principles, insights, phrases and information and write them down individually on A5 cards.

The cards you place now on places where you always stop, such as on the bathroom mirror, on the refrigerator or in your car. Read it through several times a day and make your thoughts about it.

In addition, it is very helpful if you carry a card with you every day and you explicitly deal with this motto.

Follow your discipline!

Yes! This means a lot of initiative and work. Any athlete will tell you that without daily disciplined workouts, muscle gaining no progress. No pain no gain!

Thus, be open for it. Take the time to invest in yourself. All the work you invest in you benefits you and your development. That is the best investment you can make.

In addition, it is very helpful if you carry a card with you every day and you explicitly deal with this motto.

Learning is a gift

You are a sum of what you learn in your life.
No matter how old you are, man create with his abilities and talents in such a way that from the beginning of his existence he always and everywhere deals with learning.

What a wonderful gift we got into our genes. Learning something new means breaking new ground, opening unknown worlds and awakening new passions. Learning is the essence of life.

Have lots of fun with it!

The 5 main guiding principles, findings from this chapter are:

Eternally destructive myths & facts

Let us take a closer look at women. I cannot help rolling up myths and facts, which are completely against the grain for women, but still regarded by society as coherent and given.

Women - the weak sex...

How many times have I heard this claim in the past and even today? Well noted primarily pronounced by men, this opinion holds firmly in the society. It is important to point out essential facts. Yes, it is correct: we women are a lot weaker than the man is because of our physical constitution. Luckily! Would men prefer them to be carried over the threshold by the woman? Probable not!

Actually, we women love this striking difference. We know that we are physically inferior to the men. By nature, it is so given that the man is the hunter while the women take care of the fire. The Neanderthals showed this well and humanity could only secure the survival of his race by this clear predetermined rules.

We women are aware of our subtlety and difference and, in principle; we do not want to change that at all. And yet...
... Do we tend to break these millennia of established, clear natural law with bending and breaking?

Oh yes, we women do ... What are some thousand years of clearly regulated laws of nature? For the last 60-70 years, women in Western civilization have been extremely successful in washing the status of the weak sex off their skin.

Why? Because women reject this opinion as an unacceptable statement, because they do not consider it correct. Here, women show a unique willpower and use it skilfully to clarify this error! For what? While women on the one hand long for security, security and a strong shoulder - and look for a strong partner - they reject it at the same time.

Why? Because women reject this opinion as an unacceptable statement, because they do not consider it correct. Here, women show a unique willpower and use it skilfully to clarify this error! For what? While women on the one hand long for security, security and a strong shoulder - and look for a strong partner - they reject it at the same time.

What a confusion! This more than clearly reflects the lack of understanding with which today's women are confronted. Since it is more than understandable that the men's world can no longer follow this emotional and mental chaos.

Superwoman

Which of us women does not want to be a superwoman? Would you like to be able to use the flies for yourself? Does this unbridled force want to know for itself, with which tons of cars are transported from A to B, without their complexion being damaged and with their beaming smile, all spectators win for themselves?

This feminine fictional character, unlike Superman, found his way onto the big screen much later. While Superman had been rescuing the earth since 1947 and just dreamed of Superwoman, Superwoman did not have the honour to get her own movie until much later.

This is in contrast to the reality where women worldwide become heroes repeatedly, in other words prove their status as superwoman over again. This is presented for example, in the documentary films of the Second World War, where women dug their hands through the rubble and rebuilt the European cities with sweat. Not to forget that even the most delicate body of women manages, as if by magic, to make a new person grow and thrive in them. After months of pregnancy, the exhausted bodies then squeeze the painful pain of sacrifice into a perfect little body of their own and look with admiration on their work, which miraculously originated in their bodies. Ladies... Be aware of the following fact:
Each one of you is truly a superwoman!

What are the roles of the woman?

The whole social and life model of the Western and the Third World would not work if the women did not exercise the numerous roles. The different role functions span from daughter, sister, wife, cook, mother, earner, and secretary to lover, girlfriend and much more. Have you ever considered how many roles you actually cover?

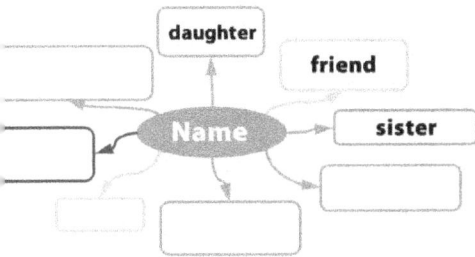

Have serious thoughts about this: In which functions are you moving? Use the mind map system by taking a blank A4 sheet and writing your name in the middle. Then you write all those features around your name that come to your mind. List them in the lower lines below.

_____

_____

In how many roles did you recognize yourself? If it is less than five, I ask you to do this exercise again. Believe me; you fill out more than five rolls! How do you feel now that you realize that you are more than "just" a woman, mother and wife?

_____

_____

Important to you and your development in this process is the fact that you draw a conclusion from your consideration. Now I invite you to draw a conclusion from this exercise for you. What conclusion do you draw from your considerations?

_____   **Summary
Result**

The role of women in today

You had trouble finding your roles. This is unusual. Many women are not aware of their multi-tasking mission. Thus, her area of responsibility grew steadily and thus increased unconsciously in quantity, without the woman even being aware of it.

Let's see what the main roles are basically. From the aspect of the family the woman is first and foremost a daughter and thus as a child the mirror of her parents. Not infrequently, the father sees in the family model his daughter as a princess, showering her with great love and at the same time gives her the feeling of being something very special and unique. This is very important and does the soul very well. However, it is also decisive whether the daughter is also shown limits and even more goals in this phase of growing up, which the child must adhere to and at the same time strive for. As a result, it learns to accept challenges and consistently strive for them.

In addition to the roles of the sister, niece, granddaughter and aunt, the life partner and the role of the wife is the next major role. In this role, the woman plays a crucial role that has an extreme impact on the environment. Be this directly within your own family, as well as in the neighbourhood, circle of friends and in the circle of acquaintances. The attitude of the wife, wife and partner reflects on the man and is inevitably reflected in the two living conditions again.

! The woman in this leading role is much more than "*just*" a wife. An important function the woman is holding is the one of the manager of the family business (ie home), who in society is paid much less or even no value and appreciation.

What a farce and a joke at the same time. When we compare the family business with a business enterprise, it quickly becomes clear what a real miracle the woman is doing at home. As a Facility Manager, the woman provides for the continuous cleaning of the house, as a food & beverage manager, she ensure a full refrigerator and fresh delicious tasting dinner while practicing as a mediator for the house peace with the sometimes-difficult neighbours. As a trustee she also ensures the timely completion of taxes, in which no separate item for any payments of these extra services of the family business appear. Why? Woman works also free of charge. Everything for the benefit of the family!

It becomes exciting for women, in addition to the role of the mother, which is now tailored to the parents as a life role. For many women, the baby fulfils a heart's desire that sweeps away every effort and pain as soon as one smiles at one's own flesh. That the work with this miracle is not less, women know very well.

With child and cone then the functions of the babysitter, educator, nurse, motivator, teacher and visionary are added, trying to pave the way for his child children early in the university.

Add to that the main role of the lover. While inevitably the 24-hour continuous use as a mother demands his attributes sooner or later, this once beloved and also with fervour played role of the beloved moves more and more into the rear. Although exactly that man was chosen as the true and only soul partner and father of the children, not infrequently finds the woman after years of rushed but so well organized family management as a single and as a single mother again. The reasons for that are complex. The result is and remains the same:

This role as a single mother was not planned!

In this concept of functions, I have not yet listed the professional world of work. However, it is this - I think - for women to take into account indispensable role. Especially if the case of the "dismissal" from the free guidance of the family business occurs by the partner moves his ways, it is crucial for the woman, if and how woman until then could position and establish professional. A work certificate from the family entrepreneur, where she has worked for many years as a manager, has hitherto had no place in our society, let alone in the world of work. Instead, the economy does not pay the gaps on a resume to respectable family management, but criticizes this gap, since women were not in the professional practice during those years.

And yet ... Slowly but surely positive changes are recognizable on the horizon. It is important to me that as a woman you realize how versatile you are on the road. How efficient, energetic and indispensable you and the women are for families, the environment and the world.

What would the world look like without women?
When this question is raised, women tend to be more likely than not to wave them off as if they were ashamed of their attention. Meanwhile, this question is actually an important one and I invite you to write down your spontaneous thought such as: What does the world look like without us women?

_____

_____

Is not it unbelievable how much our focus changes, how our view sharpens, if we direct our vision to the essentials? You should refrain from any false modesty, but choose the answer from the perspective of the third party. This provides for neutral viewing and - most importantly - for a new and in-depth view.

**Summary
Result**

Now I invite you to draw a conclusion from this exercise for you. Say, what do you take from this consideration? What did you learn from it?

_____

Difference between man and woman
"We cannot be with them, but we cannot be without them," we hear ourselves say as an exclamation of despair over the men. However, it is true that we women love men the way they love us. It is one of the laws of life that people need each other, because, among other things, one hand is much easier to handle than if the man or woman pulls

alone. Among other things, in the book "*Mars loves Venus, Venus loves Mars*" the differences between man & woman are treated in detail. If you have not read the book yet, I highly recommend this reading to you.

In the run-up, we took a closer look at the woman and her roles. I would like to motivate you to think about males.

> What are the differences from your point of view? In which areas are men supporting women? What do you like about the men? What qualities do you appreciate about them? What advantages do you see in them? Write spontaneously what you can think of, value-free and without much thought.

_____

_____

Choose from your collected and recorded points your 3 main points that you appreciate about the men:

1. _____

2. _____

3 _____

What is your conclusion from this?

_____

What is a thoroughbred woman?
> When the *word thoroughbred woman* falls, in many minds the associations of spirited, well-known female faces automatically run like a movie. So *Monica Bellucci, Gina Lollobrigida, Sophie Loren* or *Marilyn Monroe* reappear in the embodiment of a real

thoroughbred woman. All these women have one thing in common: they are racy, spirited, and beautiful and have a unique charisma, and ... also a touch of infamy!

Does the woman of today have to meet those standards to go through as a thoroughbred woman? Is it a compliment or an insult when a man calls a woman a full-blooded woman? What is understooden as a thoroughbred woman?

During my research I often came across this question. Just put by men, it was quite an uncertainty of understanding because. This shows the tendency for men to associate the word thoroughbred woman with a woman who is an angel in the kitchen and a devil in bed.

This moved me to interview women and men and to incorporate the results of my internet research in my personal interpretation. In summary, I came to the following conclusion:

A thoroughbred woman is...

...a woman who lives with body and soul the woman-being and feels as a woman with all the attributes. She is proud of it and presents it with dignity, appreciation and gratitude. She is totally attached to her body no matter how pronounced her curves are. She carries an attractive (life) joy in her, which reflects her in her movements like an inexhaustible field of energy. She dresses authentically, has her own style and plays her charms in a graceful and elegant way, but they are not intrusive. She knows exactly what she wants and at the same time approaches the matter with determination and cautiousness.

Athoroughbred woman is aware of the irresistible effects of her stimuli and uses them whenever she wants; but not in a disreputable way. It jumps - to the annoyance of many - not immediately with everyone to bed, despite persistent and consistent attempts. On the contrary. The thoroughbred woman is picky, very picky! In addition, patient at the same time. She wants to be conquered and is extremely romantic. Knowing exactly what an exceptional and desirable woman she is, she thoroughly values esteem, respect and attention.

Rightly so, because a thoroughbred woman is passionate, enjoyable and very active and at the same time gives her chosen one the same appreciation and full attention. In addition, she is fully alive with both legs, is very self-confident, sociable, and successful professionally and can express himself well in the male world. She is popular with women and men and knows exactly what she wants!

A thoroughbred woman does not become that type because of her looks, but her attitude to being a woman is crucial. This attracts both man and woman at the same time. Femme fatale pure!

Do you feel attracted or repelled by her? Or does the description in you awaken the desire to be that self-confident woman who is unwavering and determined in her own way.

_____

_____

Do you recognize parallels to you? How much thoroughbred woman do you think you carry in yourself? How much full-blooded woman do you live already?

_____

Here I have good news for you: You carry this woman in you! Yes exactly! You are already this woman. Every cell in your body is a woman through and through. You are completely a woman, have all these attributes in you. These are in front of you, inside you, waiting for you to live them completely. As well as you all women of this world carry these wonderful qualities in themselves.

Are you wondering why you do not feel like a full-blooded woman then, rather than perceiving and seeing you? In the following

29

chapters, you will recognize and understand more about this.

If you cannot or do not want to identify with this form of definition, then I can understand that. However, this fact cannot be denied by the fact that you, as a woman, have been given these genes in the cradle. You can continue to reject this from you. Keep in mind that ignorance does not mean that you are a woman. Nevertheless, it remains part of you.

Of course, it is entirely up to you which of your universe-given wonders you'd like to use effectively from your backpack. The more support you accept, the better and easier it is. I should be added, that the skills wither away when they are not used. Like a muscle. If this is not trained, it is steadily smaller, weaker and unloaded. However, this does not disappear. He remains in his small, weak form, alert and ready. For you, that means you can always access and retrieve this ability. In the beginning, it will be a little bumpy, but with mindfulness and the appropriate training, your femininity will be taken out of the sun and you will be enormously strengthened in your womanhood.

What is your conclusion from this?

**Summary
Result**

_____

Femininity - a taboo?

?

Femininity is an indispensable trademark in many cultures, such as in Japan, where Geisha women is the epitome of femininity. At that time like today. In our Western world, femininity is much discussed and discussed. This is proven by the numerous books that deal extensively with this interesting topic.

What exactly does femininity mean? For many people, femininity is recognizable in the form of an outward appearance. High-heeled shoes, pouty lips with red lipstick are placed in the foreground and also the wild mane is interpreted by men as female expression.

Women questioned place higher demands on their own gender, although differences are also visible. While one group justifies this in the outer packaging, that is, in the female curves and the way of clothing, the other group sees this more in a deeper sense. This is understood by the feeling and acting out of the most different feelings that the woman in her femininity carries as a result of the whole outward. An interesting aspect that I would like to explain in more detail.

What are the feelings we talk her about? Clearly, trust is one of those strong emotions. This is guided by the knowledge, trust that everything is going well. I interpret this as the basic trust in us. From this knowledge, basic trust that everything is and is good, caring and maternal build up in the woman. A woman does not necessarily have to be a mother to live her motherhood.

The nourishing love that women carry in us based on our original trust is a good thing that surrounds us with a loving aura. This form of love is perceived by humans and animals and is attractive. Women have a wisdom in us that we inherited from our ancestors. I recognize this as a precious gift and gift that women, with our femininity as ability, have been given in their lap. The knowledge of this power is valuable. Our intuition as a channel speaks to us and gives us clues that, together with the basic trust, are very clear guideposts. This ability of intuition also carries men into it. However, because of their basic trust and wisdom, women are better trained in dealing with this. However, it is true that women of the Western world were more likely to wither this ability, and we use this gift only to a limited extent. Fortunately, this is available at any time.

Our femininity finds its breeding ground in nature, where it is at home and recharges energy. That is why it is important for us women to connect with nature, Mother Earth. This is a deep buried need that nourishes us. Another expression of femininity is the desire to express yourself individually. Expressing our emotions in the form of dancing, movement, creative action such as painting or singing is

31

essential to us. This includes the physical act of sex. Each of these actions is an expression of femininity, which is weaker or stronger depending on access.

How do you feel about your femininity?

Every woman faces her femininity individually. While some deal with their femininity and live it out, the others ignore it completely.

Do you want to know how you feel about it? Question yourself: note in which form you express your femininity. Think about it in peace. If it does not flow at first, do not be too strict with yourself. The more often you question yourself, the more it flows.

_____

_____

Think about the form in which you can imagine a deepening of being a woman. How can you express this? Acting out?

_____

_____

What steps, actions and changes will you initiate in order to feel and experience your femininity more intensively?

1. _____

2. _____

3. _____

What did you learned about your own femininity?

Summary Result

_____

The 5 main guiding principles, findings from this chapter are:

Do you have lust for … ?

Lust is a much-discussed topic. In most cases, it is spoken about the sexual pleasure. The Internet is heaped with debates about the pros and cons of lust mostly in combination with the desire for sex. In this respect, I refer to pleasure in general, questioning the importance and significance of pleasure as a whole.

Epicurus and his doctrine of lust

I cannot help but imagine Epicurus, a philosopher of antiquity, who went down in history for his doctrine of lust. Even then, this issue was extremely sensitive and so Epicurus was labelled, as a pleasure pig, as his teachings were related to the desire for sex. Wrongful, for Epicurus, with his teachings, referred to nature and its legislation, which in the wider sense led to ethics.

In doing so, Epicurus pointed out that everything is heading for two principles. On the desire, on the one hand aspired & the achievement as a goal and on the other hand refers to the pain, which should be avoided. With pain Epicurus neither means sadomaso techniques nor the pain caused by extreme sexual activities. Instead, the philosopher referred to quite natural sensations such as the extreme feeling of hunger, thirst, anxiety or physical sensation of pain.

Epicurus goes into depth to assert that adequate and bearable pain inevitably leads to a higher sense of pleasure. In doing so, the human being accepts this pain when the target is clearly targeted. Any marathon runner can sing a song about it. A prima ballerina forgets her blistered foot pain as soon as she twists a perfect pirouette at the performance. The woman forgets the painful hours of childbirth as soon as she finally holds her baby in her arms.
The feeling of happiness simply dominates.

Once the person has reached his goal, all pain is forgotten and only the triumphant feeling of joy, happiness dominates. All pain is fit. The only thing that matters is happiness and elation. Strictly speaking, the little seed of *"lust for more ..."* is already back in its infancy through this sense of happiness. New goals and visions are emerging. Despite all the pain and sacrifice.

But not only in antiquity, but also in modern times, dedicate many writers, scientists and artists their time and studies the subject of lust. Among other things, created a variety of sayings and common phrases that are used to our modern times.

- *"Lust shortens the way"* (William Shakespeare)
- *"Imagination is the greatest pleasure gain"* (Damaris Wieser)
- *"Lust a drop that does not quench your thirst"* (Dr. Carl Peter Fröhlich)
- *"Dear a sigh of lust, as one Sigh of frustration"* (Helga Schäferling)

One thing, however, all the sayings show:

Lust is something unique and special!

Lust is not just lust

The desire in its meaning has to offer a much larger repertoire than the category of sexuality. In the German language the idiom, *"Do you feel like it...?"* Is of great importance and use. The questioning of everyday situations outside of sexual activity is questioned. Such as: Do you want to go for a walk or a trip?

All the more exciting that with the word lust - alone - mostly in the minds of people sexuality finds its anchor. Nothing speaks against it. I go to this topic in chapter *"Do you have sexual fulfilment?"* Closer to the desire for sex. Here I would like to address the different forms of pleasure.

Because lust is not just lust.

With the statement *"I can feel a great desire for a hike through the forest"*, I define my inner yearning to know my body in the forest. I express a desire that goes hand in hand with a shortcoming. In this case, I long for rest and new energy, which I can draw from experience in the forest. With pleasure, I express thus that I feel a lack somewhere and want to know this emptiness filled. This understanding is crucial. Just for someone itself.

In the hustle and bustle of our everyday lives, we humans, men and women have the ability to feel our true lust, mostly lost. We let ourselves be distracted by the technology and forget to listen completely to our inner - our inner voice - who knows exactly what is good for our body, mind and soul.

Although women are gifted with a deeper rooting for nature than in comparison to our male colleagues, this does not mean that we can handle it better in our time. Our inner voice, which would bring us closer to our void, our shortcomings, is mostly drowned out with external irrigation (*activities that distract us, such as the Internet, etc.*).

In this context, our highly sensitive capacity for one's own perception - which would be good for us at this moment - is dazzled. In doing so, we let ourselves have a great opportunity for pleasure, be it through food, music, contact with fellow human beings. This lack of perception is an indication that energy levels are low in that area. In order to refuel it, it is necessary - in order to respond to the preceding example - to take a forest walk without a mobile phone and distraction alone.

What do we do instead? We cover the inner voice with distraction, as with work or other external influences. The shortcoming of perception thus remains.

What about your pleasure, your lust?
Now it is time to deal with your lust. We want to get this desire together now on the track.

Now ask yourself spontaneously:

What are you in the mood for now?

Practice

Lean back and feel deeply in your body. Hide foreign sounds and focus on your body and inner voice. What is it that you want you to do now?

_____

How was this exercise for you? Was it difficult for you to feel your body and call your lusts?

TIP

It is important for you to serve this ability of clearly naming your cravings at all times. This sensation is, so to speak, our own inner mouthpiece that knows exactly what it takes to make you feel completely at ease. However, if we cannot feel what we want, what our body needs to feel completely well, we are steadily moving away from the happiness that is the essence of happiness and health.

If you find it difficult to name your desire for that particular something, I invite you to practice it. This gift, this ability is just a little rusty. I advise you that you deliberately question your lust daily. Instead of automatically grabbing the fridge for the first-best, ask yourself:

What am I really in the mood for now?

The more often you become aware of your natural ability, the faster you are in direct contact with this internal communication and can provide your body with the desired things. This inevitably promotes your health, well-being and ultimately your overall happiness.

What did you recognize about your lust? What is your conclusion from this? What are your next steps?

Summary Result

_____

No lust? No desire? And now? What to do?

Are you one of those women who do not enjoy it? They do not know exactly what they want. No longer in direct contact with her body and therefore it is all the more difficult to name the thing - the true pleasure - by name. The previous exercise had led to no result for you, because you felt or felt nothing?

No worries. It is not just you. Many people carry this blank, ignorance and do not know their own needs. In this state of non-real-cognition, it happens that much more is eaten than hunger actually claims. Instead of enjoying the ignorant falls into feasting.

In fact, it is not uncommon in our time for us to have forgotten to feel, to scan, our desire. We are constantly being informed about the marketing wave via TV, internet, radio and smartphone, on what we should like. Completely irrelevant if this is really true. Our mind takes these suggestions as true and lets them seduce us.

This begins in the morning as soon as we drive by car past a billboard and ends in the evening in front of the TV, where a promotional clip of a delicious chocolate ice cream is presented to us. Out of 10 people, 7 get up and get a treat, although their belly is still much filled from dinner.

The question is: How do you escape this rat's tail, which happens daily in front of your nose? The good news is that you have already gone halfway through recognizing this fact alone. Bravo! The second half is to resist all these temptations. Instead, learn to ask yourself critically whether your body really craves chocolate.

**Practice in the critical questioning yourself,
in listening and in feeling inside of you and
the clear understanding of yourself!**

Especially we women are trapped in the trap of time. We are replete with endless agenda items summed up in a meticulous schedule. Far too rarely are time buffers scheduled, which gives these types of queries freedom.

TIP

Practice

Start today with 5 to 10 minutes of daily time.
At this time, you are reporting with your body and communicating with it. By giving yourself this time, you are taking the first step towards a neutral and liberated cognition and decision on your desires.

Every day before sleeping, ask yourself how many times you have succeeded in discovering your desires, lusts, sensations.

It is best to write this every evening in your lucky journal and get an overview of your progress. **This is important!** This is how you perceive your development. The more often you perform the exercise, the easier it will be for you.

Write down now 3 measures with which you begin the daily practice of this exercise from now on.

1. _____

2. _____

3. _____

Well done

39

The 5 main guiding principles, findings from this chapter are:

The way to a fulfilled relationship

Humans care following the behaviour of a herd animal in itself. We prefer loneliness to the company of other people. This is reflected in all cultures where people - be it in the city or on land in all parts of the globe - live together in smaller or larger groups. There are people who prefer solitude and lead a hermit life. This is rarely the result of negative experiences that group life has with people.

In addition to these types of companies, people in us strive for the intense desire to find our Mr. or Ms. Right. The clear goal is to find the person we are looking for - the so-called matching lid - to lead a harmonious and happy partnership. Many people believe that they can only be happy when this person finally enters their lives. Do you believe that too?

Where are you currently standing?
In what situation are you currently? Are you in a happy, harmonious relationship that fills you up completely? Are you a single out of conviction or out of necessity? A single mother trying after a failed marriage along with household, work and education from time to time at the exit with friends to have fun. You will often find yourself looking for Mr. Right.

Practice

I like to invite you to define your current situation:

I_____

_____

_____

Please remember that it is not about valuation. There is no right or wrong, but only your sensation, your feeling. It is crucial in every situation to know how you are doing. Ask yourself further:

Does your situation make you happy? Do you feel alone? Are you missing something in the current situation? If yes, what? Feel inside yourself & listen to your inner voice. How do you feel?

I _____

_____

We rarely stop to listen to ourselves. Meanwhile, our body, mind and soul are constantly talking to us. The question is whether you perceive and hear these messages. These exercises invite you to listen to your inner self, to scan. Because that is important information for you and your well-being.

Therefore, consider: What is your conclusion from this exercise? What exactly do you want? What did you learn from it?

_____

Summary Result

Where does your journey guide you?

We humans, women and men alike, tend to just run away from our lives and not even think about where we're going.

While we organize a vacation trip from day 1 to the last, we mostly fail to do so with our lives. The basic question is:

What do you want? Where should your journey take you?

It is like you want to start as the captain of your ship and call your crew to "*Put sail!*". OK! Only where is it going? In which direction is your compass aligned? Should it go to the south, north, west or east? The answer is crucial to your further steps and alignment.

There is only a limited number of lifetimes available to us all. These should be used as well as possible. That is why it is important to know which direction you're heading. Because if you are looking for the South deep in your heart, but are heading north, your call to the South has not disappeared. But on the contrary. The further you go, the more intense it becomes. Ask yourself now:

Where should your journey go? What are you striving for?

?

_____

_____

Did you have the trouble that nothing came into your mind? Did you dispute your answers? Do not worry. We will discuss this in more detail in the following chapters.

I am most important to myself ...

Are you one of those women who put themselves last, place them at the end of the line? Before you look at yourself, you let everyone precede, selflessly granting them precedence. Your husband or partner, your children, parents, as well as your work colleagues?! You do that, although you would also like to play in the front ranks. But your (mother's) instinct far too rarely allows you to give yourself the seat in the first place. The result is that your environment is completely used to your selfless behaviour. Who stays on the track?

Yes, exactly: YOU!

Oh, you mean that as a mother it is your duty to put your children first. I totally agree with you that as a mother you have the responsibility for your children. This does not mean that you have to behave like a serf.

Take time for yourself!

Treat yourself to a break from the family! The first step is your decision to give yourself that time and then demand it from your environment. Believe me; it is quite feasible for your environment. It is all a question of communication and organization. You will see: One hour for you, all alone for you, is enormously nurturing.

What would you do if you had an hour on your own every day?

_____

Does not that sound inviting? Start taking this lesson today! It is up to you and your decision.

_____

May I introduce: "My Mr. Right ..."

Often I hear women complaining *"Where is my Mr. Right?"*. There is something crucial to clarify in advance: HOW your Mr. Right should be? What features should he be equipped with. I agree! It is like goal setting. Only if you know where the journey is going, you can align the radar accordingly.

TIP

I invite you to capture your secret ideas of your Mr. Right here. **It is YOUR wish partner!** So forget all the rules and standards. What should this man look like? What qualities should he have? What profession is he pursuing? Does he have kids? How old is he? Is he divorced? Where he lives? What is his past? Does he have money? Is he successful? What hobbies are his passions? Does he like cooking? Is he faithful? Is he loving? Etc.

Create your Mr. Right by describing him as explicitly as possible. Take an A4 sheet and start:

Practice

_____

_____

_____

When I first thought seriously about my Mr. Right and I kept my preferences on paper, I reworked the draft for 3 weeks until I finally held the final version in my hand.

Take your time! Do not stress, but think well, like how your Mr.

Right - you from now on your side want to know - should be. It is your Mr. Right, he is allowed to and he should be up to your wishes.

But beware: **Be careful what you wish!** Think about exactly what features and facts your Mr. Right brings. For those who want to delve deeper into this topic, I recommend my book *"Lust ... to meet your Mr. Right?"*.

I want to grow old with my partner...
Suppose you are in a relationship and have a long-time partner by your side. Ask yourself: Is he your fulfilment? Does this person correspond to your Mr. Right? Do you love him? Would you like to grow old with him? If so, I congratulate you! It is wonderful to know someone by his side who is the perfect lid to his pot.

However, most women will answer this question with a clear or hesitant "no." Whereby it must be distinguished. It is one thing to love a man and another, whether you want to grow old with your life partner. These are two fundamentally different things and I really invite you to consider this as a difference as well. How I mean this?

Many relationships are out of habit, for the sake of convenience or because of the children together. It is irrelevant for what reasons you are with your partner. What matters is if you can imagine being with this man until the end of your days. Drop all conventions and think about this.

The following exercise is instructive: Take your current age. In my case, this is 49 years. One study shows that in women the average life expectancy is 84 years and in men 79 years.

Practice

Thus, statistically speaking, I still have a total of 35 years, which is equivalent to **12740 days.**

Twelve thousand seven hundred and forty days!

A number that inevitably gets smaller every day. It is important that you realize how much time you have left. Lifetime is and remains limited. Already at birth, this law was clearly clear. At the same time, death was given to each of us at the same time as life. Especially in the Western time we like to forget this, displace this fact. But now you imagine this fact. Now you calculate those days of life you statistically still have to live. What comes out of you?

My statistically remaining days are_____

How do you feel when you realize this number? Does this number seem puny to you? Do you realize how valuable every day of life is? All the more important every day to make the best.

So ask yourself: Do you want to spend your remaining …. days (see above) with your current partner?

_____

Why are you together with your partner?

I invite you now with my provocative questions to be honest with you. After all, it is about something very important: **Your life!**

So ask yourself the following questions: Why are you dating your partner? What is the reason? Is it love? Because of the habit? Are you scared to hurt him and your environment? Because of children? The fear to be alone? Afraid to find another man? To stay?

_____

_____

Be honest and open to yourself!

Do not blame yourself, but bring the truth to the point. Even when it hurts. It is crucial for you and your future!

Better of alone, as then to be as a couple alone

In our western world, being alone is a way of life that is seldom voluntarily sought. While the Native American tribes assume aloneness as a fixed life-ritual, in Western culture we tend to accept aloneness more as a disliked state rather than as a nourishing, instructive time. This view is supported by social opinion and behaviour.

Meanwhile, being alone, this time where you are only dealing with yourself, has an incredible enriching energy in it, which, if accepted positively, will carry you a great deal. Despite this knowledge, many women tend to stay in a pattern of staying in a relationship that does not make them happy, rather than being alone. The children, the environment - what do the neighbour's say - or just because of their own fear.

I was alone many times. I travelled alone through many countries all over the world and always found myself in the best company by meeting wonderful people who accompanied my street for some time. The wonderful thing about being alone is the options that grow from it. Being on the road alone makes you more alert, creative and, above all, happier. It also brings you closer to yourself, as it gives you time, space and silence to engage with yourself.

The question is what makes up more? Your fear to be alone? Or the idea of what and who will cross your path as soon as you decide to be alone? The new situation changes your perspective and so does your perception. You will recognize things and people that you cannot see with the severity of your current situation as you take a different attitude and perspective.

_____

_____

Everything has its price! As Epicurus has stated in his doctrine of pleasure and brought to the point: It requires a path of pain that will inevitably lead to higher pleasure. So also in relation to your wish life. To experience this complete pleasure, you have to skip some hurdles before.

One is too much within a love triangle

I know many women who are stuck in a love triangle. The role of the second wife is an ungrateful. The uninterrupted duality between the deep love that is felt for this one man - even though he is married or otherwise involved - and the intense desire to know the heart man on his own is an uninterrupted tightrope walk because of secrecy and unfulfilled longing.

Certainly, a triangular relationship has its advantages too.
The partner comes in the best of humour to his lover, spoils them and opens to her honest and open. The wife usually does not know anything about her rival. Not infrequently, the second wife is a good friend of the family and invited to family celebrations. As a result, the rival often carries the bitter aftertaste of this constellation around even more.

? If you live in a love triangle, I invite you to ask yourself why you chose this relationship. A provocative question? How do you feel in this constellation? What are your intentions? How long are you willing to sustain and lead this relationship? Does your lover match your ideas of your Mr. Right, who you share with another woman?

_____

_____

Please be honest with yourself. It does not matter what others say. If you are happy in this relationship, then this is wonderful for you.

However, I would like to invite you to critically question your inner self and let it speak. It is about your life, about your remaining days in life.

48

Are you ready to live your remaining days of life (...?) like this?

Pets as a substitute

Especially women tend to take a pet. Not infrequently to facilitate being alone and to fill the emptiness that they feel in their single life. Having a pet is something wonderful. As soon as the front door is opened the lady is greeted by her dog. The animal is immensely happy and shares its joy with no ifs or buts. What a feast for a mistress who is happy about this attention, emotional outburst. She feeds on it. Thinking it over, was she ever welcomed by her ex-deceased in this way? No!

In addition, it proves to be practical that the animal bluntly sniffs at men while walking and separates the litter from the wheat. Practically! Clearly, Mr. Right is one thing the female pet owners say: A dog lover! If the beloved animal can smell the new man by your side, that is a positive sign for the female dog owner. Doggie knows it just out there.

In this constellation, it should be noted that this love of animals should not become a substitute for the partner. In many cases, one half of the bed is filled by the Golden Retriever and cuddled with the owner. In some cases, a second pet is added to the first pet, and mum loses more and more ground in her own bed and house.

Also popular is the attitude of cats in women. Cat lovers tick differently than the dog owners. The dog must be led to a walk, while the cat is her own master. She goes where and when she wants. Mistress is seen by the four-paw more than feeder and for cuddling is quite acceptable. Otherwise, the hangover or sweet kitten cannot say anything. She is her own boss and lives accordingly. Women holding cats have found an interim solution. While cats kept in the city have been raised to pets - in the truest sense of the word - cats living on land are closer to their origin. They explore nature and return to the house after their Crusades and their liking.

Why does a woman keep a pet? Pure animal love? Partner replacement? Children replacement? Filling in the void?

Are you a pet owner? Do you keep a dog or cat?
I gladly invite you to question your motives for animal husbandry. Of course you love your pet. That is out of the question. Now ask yourself what motivations you hold an animal. What do you compensate for that? For all ladies who do not have a pet, you also question why you do not keep a pet?

Practice

_____

_____

Our environment reflects ourselves, our interior.

Mostly we do not recognize this. That is why the next exercise is exciting. You have either a cat or a dog. Which species is this? Small, big? What are the characteristics of this animal? Rather caring or aggressive? Is it more independent or familial? Why did you choose this species? If you do not have a pet, what kind of animal would you choose? How about your pet?

_____

_____

Yes, your pet is your mirror. What do you recognize in your description? What does your pet reflect on you? Do you carry the character traits of your pet in you as well? What does this animal (real or fictional) say about you and your life?

_____

_____

What has the one thing to do with the other? I will show you ...

Mirror, mirror on the wall...

Unmistakable and fascinating are the parallels that our environment shows and we reflect in them. The mirror resonance! When we are mindful, we recognize in our environment the answers we seek. However, we have forgotten this - men and women alike. What's up with the mirror resonance?

You look in the mirror. What do you see? What do you recognize? Your beauty? Your perfectly shaped face? Or do you recognize your blemish that - in your opinion - in the small nose, the wrinkles around your eyes and thin lips present.

What's happening? Basically, your reflection shows you a neutral, worthless picture of something. If you look in, you recognize yourself in it - logical, right? The mirror has no further task than to mirror what the counterpart indicates.

The mirror does not interpret, but reflects (only).

It gets exciting when the viewer includes his evaluation. Is he seeing the seeing as beautiful or unpleasant? Therein lies the key:

It is always in the eye and in the utilization of the observer, how he perceives something.

Let us do an experiment? Here we go...
What do you see when you look in the mirror? What kind of woman is looking at you? Is she smiling? Are her eyes full of energy? What is your appearance? Does she look happy? What kind of charisma do you perceive?

Practice

_____

_____

What did you write down? Are you surprised about the result? Be aware about following:

Your description is exactly what you think about you!

The interpretation of what you see in the mirror says a lot about you and your opinion about you. Of course, it depends on your daily form. This inevitably influences your own view. However, it remains unchanged, as you accept it. How do you look at yourself, with care, with love? Do you stroke yourself with a look full of appreciation or do you badly go into critically court with yourself?

Practice

Another exciting mindfulness exercise is by smiling on the streets. People will look at you in wonderment, look around in confusion, wondering at the same time if they know you, and ... That is the amazing thing! You will be greeted warmly by unknown passersby. Especially the elderly and children are extremely alert and respond quickly to your smile. Is not it nice when unknown people smile at you with a smile?

You alone decide how to perceive and accept yourself in the mirror. Perception carries with it the word "*take*".

The result: Gratefully just accept yourself as you are. **It is just the way you are, because you're a wonderful, unique, fantastic person!**

What do you take with you out of this lesson?

Who loves me...?

Women tend to get affirmations for love in the outside. From our family, parents, siblings, from our partner. The problem with this constellation and expectation is that you cannot decide how and what the other thinks. Whether your mother loves, you depends on her and not on you. Whether your father recognizes you as a daughter is not your call, but your father's.

Although this is understandable in itself, we often find ourselves in the most impossible models of thinking. It fights for the attention of the parents like a lion. You spend endless amounts of energy trying for decades to make people aware of what a unique daughter or son they have. The disappointment is painful if this is not returned despite the infinite attempts.

> The same model continues with the partner. As a woman, we feel obliged to ensure that the blessing does not hang crooked, but just hangs - that is, harmonious. How often does each individual dislocate in this effort?

Therefore: Always remember that as a human being and a woman you should not mislead others, even if they are still so close to you, but accept you as you are. It is indispensable that you overwhelm yourself with a lot of love, mindfulness and appreciation. Do not put this task in the hands of others, only in yours.
Again, only in yours!

As soon as you give up this responsibility, you open up the possibility that you will be kicked with words and deeds. You do not deserve that because you are a unique person with extraordinary skills and talents. **Love yourself totally.**

Tell yourself what a wonderful person you are every day. Write this in your Happiness Journal (*page 170*) for how beautiful, wonderful, and extraordinary you are. Look for reference points, say confirmations that support your claim. We humans are mind-controlled and therefore need evidence to substantiate our mental claims.

Search for at least 3 reference points each day reflecting your love. **Remember that your environment is your mirror.** Thus, your love is reflected in your environment. What do you see? What do you recognize?
Did someone smile at you today? Did you receive a compliment? What did people tell you today? Note these experiences. The more

Practice

often you do that, the more you will see what happens around you. What happened to you today in this situation, everything wonderful?

_____

_____

_____

_____

The beginning of a fulfilled relationship is to totally love, appreciate and respect yourself. No matter what your partner or what others say about you.

The key is your SELF- LOVE!

So ask yourself: Is there someone who loves me?
Oh yeah…

I love myself!

Summary Result

What do you take with you out of this lesson?

_____

_____

_____

_____

The 5 main guiding principles, findings from this chapter are:

Do you follow your call...

We all are carrying a purpose in us. The call for our purpose, for our individual life task! This call is only very weakly perceived in one person, while in others it sounds loud. This explains the phenomenon when a child exclaims at a young age that it wants to become a doctor and does it naturally in adult life. This child had clearly perceived his inner call and could thus exclude all other options without discussion and ad-act.

Occupation = Vocuation

As illustrated by the example of the child, each person carries his own unique vocation. The question is this: When will he or she become aware of it?

Our school system as well as universities have not paid too much attention to the exploration of the vocation either at all or only to a limited extent. As a result, adolescents become disgruntled adults who engage in a profession that has nothing to do with their (her) calling. Why? No focus and attention was on exploring their individual vocation. What a severe development that affects the well-being of the person.

People who recognize their inner calling, follow their calling, pursue it in their professional lives, are far happier, happier and more balanced people than those who take over the paternal business due to family constellations, even though their call to the career of a pianist cries.

In most cases, people do not recognize their inner reputation, their vocation. In our Western society, no rituals are integrated that deal with this important issue. For Indian tribes, it was necessary for any young person to retire to the forest for days to meditate on his higher I. In this encounter, you will find answers to crucial questions that point the young person in his direction. In the Western world can address these fundamental issues by dealing more vigorously and more focused with this important topic. Especially for mothers certainly provides a wonderful platform. By attentively observing your child, interrogating preferences, and showing him the widest range of possibilities, you assist your child in filtering out and recognizing his (her) calling. Your child will discover his calling faster and can follow it.

What you do for a living…?

Do you practice a profession that fills you? Who makes you happy in a nourishing way? Which leads you into a flow state?

No?! Perhaps it will comfort you to know that well over 80% of employees in our Western society are dealing with a profession that does not make them happy. They followed in the footsteps of their ancestors to meet the family's wishes. That may make the family happy, but are the needs of the person affected covered?

You spend over a third of your day working on your work. Does this make you happy? If not, this can usually lead to declining health, heartbreak and depression, unhappiness and a great emptiness.

Consider your situation. How much do you love your job? Do you feel deep in yourself that it is your vocation? Do you have the desire for a new job? Do you want to run your own company, but have not had the courage to do so yet? How much do you feel about your job? What thoughts do you come up with?

Practice

_____

_____

Summary Result

What is your conclusion? Do you lead a profession that matches your reputation and calling? What do you learn from this?

_____

Are you living your vocation?

Did the previous exercise show that you are one of those 80% of people who do not live up to their vocation? Or worse ... I do not even know it.

Be aware that you are like a multitude of people. You have no idea what her vocation is. Maybe they have a hunch, maybe a guess, but really cannot name it by name.

For this I have two good news for you:

1. We live in a time when it is customary to practice a new profession after 10 years. What was unimaginable for our grandparents today is a thing of the past. It is thus never too late for a change. Not for you either.

2. There are good ways to recognize your vocation. Let's go back a few years.

What did you dream of as a child...?

What is natural for children is almost inconceivable for us adults. Although we used to be children ourselves, the perspective of a child seems completely removed from us as adults. Actually crazy in the truest sense of the word. All our answers are in our bones and we put them down as adults. Not quite, because your answers are still in you. Something dusty may even be buried, but still within your reach.

Think about it, what did you dream as a child? What did you want to do? What attracted you magically? Let your thoughts flow freely and write them down uncensored:

_____

_____

Give yourself time for this exercise.

It is important that you activate the trains of thought and watchfully hold on to your thoughts. It happened to me that childhood dreams came to my mind when I watched children playing in the forest. Suddenly, I saw myself in the forest as a seven-year-old, and the memories of gathering wood roots and turning them into sculptures overwhelmed each other.

TIP

Get used to the fact that you always carry a block and scribe with you. Thus, you can capture your thoughts, flashes and memories. As fast as they come they are gone so fast.

What do you like to do?

You will receive information about what you liked to do as a child. Your current life gives you numerous signs that you will now deal with. Our call is shown in small facets, such as in the pursuit of hobbies.

What do you like to do in your free time? Cook? To paint? Is constructing part of your passion? Do you invent children's stories? What do you like to do?

_____

_____

To deal with things and activities that give us inner pleasure and satisfaction is unmistakably an indication of our very individual call. Being aware of your favourite pastimes is an important step that can lead you to your vocation as well.

Use your strengths and talents

You did not have certain talents in the cradle for no reason. Your talents are comparable to custom software systems that steer your hardware in the right direction. Equipped with this software, you can bring certain programs, goals efficiently & with ease in the gears. If used.

It is frightening how few people are aware of their strengths and talents. On the other hand, they can list their weaknesses down to the last detail. At the same time, the focus should be on the strengths in every livelihood, on what reinforces.

Practice

Ask yourself: Do you know your strengths? Are you aware of them? Do you know what you are good at? Where are your talents? How do you differentiate yourself from other people?

_____

_____

Did this exercise show you tapping in your own ignorance? You do not know your own strengths & do not quite know what makes you different from other people? If so, try the following:

TIP

Step 1: Ask what others appreciate about you.
What qualities and strengths do you like about you? Which of your character traits do you find particularly great? What do you appreciate about you? What would they trust you with?

_____

_____

It is always a great gift to experience what other people think about you. Of course, you really only ask people who you appreciate and respect. Preferably, you choose people from your friends, work and family. Make sure that family members are somewhat biased, while good friends see you from a more neutral perspective.

Step 2: Which activities are easy for you?
Surely you've noticed that you can do things quicker and easier than others. What kind of activities are these? Write down those activities that do not bother you.

_____

Just things that are easy for you - such as crafting - is an indication that a talent, a talent is hidden. Watch yourself & know what you are good at.

These key points are to be brought to you by the point. This is rather difficult, because things that are easy for us are nothing special for us. Others may admire us for this ability. Thus, surveys of the outside (Step 1) and your own questioning (Step 2) are a good combination that will give you valuable insights.

What do you take with you?

Summary Result

_____

Career is just for tough women...

Let's get to the point. Although we are in the twenty-first century, in many countries neither society nor the economy is focused on giving women the great career support.

Statistics in western countries confirm that the female quota in companies is still very low. In addition, women earn on average less for the same job than their male counterparts. It has been proven that women with their female skills are better at multi-tasking, faster and more efficient in their decision-making, and much more resilient than their male counterparts. Despite all these factors, on average there are few women in higher positions in the companies. Meanwhile, women are working harder to climb the career ladder, accepting more deprivations, and staying focused when it comes to achieving their goals. Not infrequently, a professionally successful woman - men and women nonetheless - hand-picked one or the other lovers 'tryst, following the idea: "_How else could she have been so successful?_"

Many women secretly want a career. Wish to start their own business, to establish oneself, to enable other women to earn an income and to create security for themselves and the family. These are clear visions that women carry deep in their hearts, but ...

unfortunately - for the most part - do not live out. Unfortunately, for herself and for the other women, who are thereby denied their chances for a better life.

Why is that so? Despite the intense emancipation movement in which thousands of women campaigned for women's rights, one of the problems for women is themselves. The focus of women is on the well-being of other people and women forget their own call for self-fulfilment. Many women try to reconcile husband, children & work. I respectfully take my hat off to these ladies who put all their energy in it! Some people manage to keep the marriage alive, the children get well educated and they can live their lives professionally.

The price is big! These women have no time for themselves & rush from one appointment to another. Their health and psyche suffer, which can often lead to burnout. A widespread phenomenon!

In addition, there are many women in their fifties who face the situation that they have either taken on low-paid part-time work or have not worked for the economy since the birth of their children to give their children full attention. Likewise, I met many women whose partners did not agree that they could live out their professional ambitions in addition to the mother role.
This disagreement does not lead to isolation sooner or later. The result of a separation is always the same: Without many years of accumulating professional experience, these women are given only limited opportunities in the economy to rehabilitate themselves.

What does this mean? **It is important that you know what you want!** That you hear and follow your call, which cries out in you for acting out, realization. It is important to perceive and live this reputation. That may be the call for the life of the fulfilled mother or the wife who is anxious only for the welfare of her husband. There is no right or wrong. It is important that you as a woman feel where you are and what is good for you.

Not to be underestimated is that needs change with age. It is one of being a mother with infants, 100% to live, savour & enjoy. When the children reach an age when caring for the wife is no longer needed 24 hrs/day, allow yourself the critical look inside. Wonder what, besides your mother role, are slumbering in you for further needs?

Allow yourself to be completely a woman!
There are many talents and abilities in you.

These must be packed up and picked up for your well-being as well as for the benefit of all people and put into action according to your inner call. Being a woman means, among other things, the many facets that you carry as a woman in you to live.

What have you learned? What do you take with you?

Summary
Result

How can I leave my family alone...?

When I talk to women, I often hear the phrase "*I cannot leave my family alone ...*". Yes, you can! Especially women who have children tend to say so and are in the trap of their sense of responsibility. To all those lady's I would like to say from the bottom of my heart that you can do that very well. Before you start as a concerned mother and wife, I would like to add that "leaving it alone" does not mean that you should go on a world tour and actually leave your family and toddlers alone for a long time.

Many women do not care much about themselves. They give all their time and attention to their family, their busy and stressed-out husband, their busy children, and other family members who complicate their daily work by complaining about the health problems of their daughter-in-law or daughter like to accept.

What remains? A woman rushing from one appointment to another. As a taxi driver in constant use for their children acts, the daily, weekly scheduling of their children has completely under control, as a club member for the annual performance of events and - of course - the family holiday from A to Z & operational implementation - including packing the entire suitcase - well planned & implemented.

Where do you stay as a woman? Do you recognize yourself? Yes, you are the family manager who has everything under control. Like any manager, you should communicate clearly to the outside world. **I am in a meeting!** In a Tête-a-Tête with an important person:

<h3 style="text-align:center">With yourself!</h3>

Treat yourself to at least 1 hour daily, which you spend all alone with you. Only with you. Not with Facebook, not with your mobile phone, not with a girlfriend, but alone with you and make this your *"Tête-a-Tête time"*. During this Tête-a-Tête period, pick up your Happiness Journal (page 170) and think about your life.

TIF

- What are your goals?
- What did you do today to achieve your goals?
- What are you grateful for?

You are the most important person in your life as a wife and mother. **It is worth your while to treat yourself for one hour a day.** Use this by going into nature, connecting with your roots, giving room to your inner voice. You will get answers to your questions.

Plan your Tête-a-Tête time into your daily routine. Communicate this with your family. Tell them that this time is very precious to you. Make the claim that your family does not bother you during this time. In this case, an open communication is important. You will see that this time will bring you much.

Your mind, heart and soul will find each other and will send you valuable messages for your next steps to self-development.

Trust in it! Do it!
When do you start with your Tête-a-Tête time?_____

Ruling

64

The 5 main guiding principles, findings from this chapter are:

How much money do you carry with you? **?**

Talking about money is a taboo in many Western cultures. On the other hand, it is necessary to present your wealth in the form of things. The aim of international advertising is to make the man feel that his 300-horsepower car is a great way to emphasize and highlight his masculinity. Even we women are seduced by international women's beauties and the created fragrances and buy them for expensive money. The motto is: *Show that you have money, even if you have none.* Having money is sexy. Having money makes you play in the upper ranks. Because of stinginess is cool. The opposite is the case!

I grew up in an environment where money was not talked about. Either you had it or not. At school, the value of an individual child was determined by the father's professional status. If this was a farmer, the child fell to a lower level. If the fathers and mothers exercised an office activity, this raised the value enormously. The top level clearly took children from entrepreneurship.

I smile about this value today. On the other hand, it is true that people continue to dismiss their own worth as valid after the assessment of the outside world. The money actually plays only a subliminal importance and is at the same time pointing. At that time like today!

How do you feel about money?
As we have noted in advance, it does not matter what others think and think about us. You have no influence on this. It also costs way too much energy to change their minds by doing educational work. Instead, use your energy by focusing on yourself, your thinking and acting. You have 100% influence on that.

Ask yourself: How do you stand for money? Do you think money is cool? Do you stand on it? Do you love money? Do you like to smell banknotes? Do you like carrying a lot of money with you? Do not think long, but intuitively write down your thoughts.

Now you have to the point, how your attitude to money is. Are you surprised about the result? What do you think about yourself after you have recorded this in black and white?

Many people are divided over the money. They need it because of the need to pay the daily costs. But like? Yes - even love?

When I first announced to the outside that I love money, incomprehensible, even suspicious glances were thrown to me. *"How can you love money ...?"* I was also asked critically and yet curious at the same time. This is exactly where the foundation of our thinking lies. We humans do not associate money as a matter in itself, but rather as a necessity, which is usually present in too little form in our lives. As something we need to pay our rent and, if necessary, to treat us to vacation. But more? Even love the money? No! We love people, animals and nature but not money?

But money is one and the same in comparison to nature. As the? **Yes, because money is actually only one and that is energy!** Just as the tree and brooks are clearly pure energy, so money is only energy in the form of atoms. Atoms that are bundled in our perception are identified as money. Just like the sea, the sky and the sun.

Recognizing and accepting money as energy is the first step in

receiving it in increased form. To balance one's self with money and this flowing energy is the step required to reshape the flow of this energy into a new form.

How do you feel about that money is just energy?

_____

Ash, coal, toads and clay

Let's take a look at how we talk about the money in general. While in English language the usage of discouraging names for money is not used, in the German language numerous other expressions such as ash, coal, toads and play dough have been found in German slang, which we use casually and coolly in terms of money. Even in dictionaries, these words are reflected in the understanding of money.

**What do all these expressions have in common?
Do you recognize it?**

The titles carry meaning and in connection with money of a rather bitter, even negative meaning. Look: The coal is used for burning and ash again. What do we do with ashes? We throw them away, we dispose of them. So when we say "_Give me the coal_ ..." we talk - albeit unconsciously - about the money to the senses that we want to burn it. We burn it, spend it. It turns to ashes.

What about the toad? Having a few toads is a colloquial synonym for having little money. This refers to the German word "_Groten_", which means groschen. Objectively, the toad is seen by most people as an ugly animal. Unlike other reptiles, a toad is not considered a pet. Instead, man goes out of the way of the toads. Be it on the road or in nature.

In other words, if we use these words for money in colloquial language, such as "_I desperately need more coal, as soon a whopping car repair bill will flutter into the house ..._" we express our intention rather than our intention - I need more money - our whole personal attitude to money to the universe again. Money is pure charcoal, what means the same means: It is only to burn. Every so often we burn the energy of the money just by using these words. The money is automatically removed from us.

And completely unknowingly!
We do not realize that we talk about the money that way. Bluntly, we adopted this use of words as part of our vernacular German.

When my coach drew my attention to my verbal use of these words in connection with money, I could not believe it. I had not noticed until then how deeply rooted that use of words in my everyday usage was in the constellation of money. Since then, I have been very conscious of my choice of words and call this energy what it is:

Appreciative and welcome energy called money!

Question your own choice of words: How is that with you? How do you call the money in your usual colloquial language?

Did you find it difficult to determine your wording? Yes? Then try the following: Record the conversation that you are making money with a friend or partner. Listen to the conversation and you will "catch" yourself acoustically as you talk about money. Ask yourself: Do I speak derogatory or appreciative of money?

The Jewish people are known for their great ability of money management and money handling. This is also evident in their language, where the money is dubbed in the nourishing word gravel, which stands for pouch. In Latin, the word Moneta - mint - handed down. From this linguistic form the English word for money is handed down.

Question: Which title will you use for money?

_____

What is your conclusion from this? What did you learn? When will you name the money what it is: **MONEY = pure energy!**

_____

Women earn less than their male counterparts

It is still common in many countries all over the world, that women to earn much less than their male counterparts. A fact that everyone is aware of. The interesting thing is that it is usually the women themselves who agree with this system and continue their good work. The economy and society build on that. Women are fundamentally polarized in that there is harmony and peace. But do not call for strife, instead choose the evil - if not approved - for peace at your own expense.

In my function as a Managing Director, I work for an international company that, like me, believes that women should earn the same rights and pay as their male counterparts. I strongly support this and motivate other companies and colleagues to do the same. I do this in line with the motto that I can bring about changes and new perspectives in my own individual area. If everyone did this in their field, the world will become different, especially for women.

These lines should motivate all women - especially in higher positions - to adopt this way of thinking. It is up to us women to positively change the position of women with our actions, our convictions and our contribution so that women all over the world can benefit from them. The more women do this, the faster this situation will change for the better for all women in the world.

Are you explicitly considering what you can do in your environment to support this? Do not underestimate your options.

Practice

_____

_____

_____

Thought is the first step. The second is to put this into action.
Start seeding today!

At what price do you sell yourself?
This title and question alone makes many women uncomfortable.
"Selling yourself...", that is not possible! Automatically, the bitter
aftertaste of prostitution comes on. However, we can still learn from
this oldest profession. The motto was and is clear: No service without
compensation!

Cross your heart! How often do women do things and work without
receiving adequate pay? Just look at the hard-working housewives
and mothers who prove this with their 24-hour busy workday. The
company owes these ladies only limited honour and respect.

As a result, women do not advertise and sell at their adequate price.
As soon as a job interview is about to mention their price, most
women are ashamed to reveal their idea. What is happening? They
sell well below their value. They do their job with more heart and
commitment than two men together and are also the last to settle for
minutes.

What ladies is going wrong here?
**It is because of the undervalued self-assessment that stands in the
way.** Only when women believe in themselves and their abilities can
they "sell" and "advertise" accordingly. Do not be too modest, lady's!

Practice How much do you praise yourself in business? Is this
analogous to your education, your knowledge? Which value is
fair?

Or in other words, how much would you like to earn?

It is good that you have said this now. How far away is your value from reality? There is a lot of teaching in our local schools and universities - from maths to writing. However, a crucial subject is lacking: **Building up and shape your self-esteem!**

Your self-esteem - as the word already implies - determines your attitude towards your true **VALUE.**

Your self-worth is reflected in your price

You yourself know best how much you are worth. But women tend to put their own value under the bushel. That is where the problem lies. While many men lean out the window in many ways, women tend to do the opposite.

How high do you estimate your self-esteem on a scale of 1 to 10, where 1 is the lowest and 10 is the highest number?

Be aware, dear colleague that this number you mentioned is far below your actual value. You are a tremendously valuable person, with incredible skills and talents.

Let this knowledge out of you! How is your environment supposed to know if you do not admit it to yourself? As discussed in advance, everything is our mirror. When a deep self-esteem dominates the person, that person wears this lesser appreciation and is visible to all.

In that sense, it is important to work on your own values and knowledge, so that you can carry it outward and that this is seen and recognized accordingly. In our own understanding of our self and our value, we are in the way of stones. They make our sale more difficult and so we accept that we are below our value on the way.

These stones are composed of different factors. These are negative experiences we have made and have anchored in our thinking as beneficial or obstructive. Likewise, the beliefs - both positive and negative - are crucial. They keep whispering to us and thus decisively determine our everyday life.

What beliefs are your spider monkeys?

Our thinking and acting is guided by so-called beliefs. Beliefs are thought patterns, programs and beliefs that we acquire throughout our lives. These differ in positive beliefs and negative ones. For example, a negative belief is "*I'm too weak to run a marathon*" while a positive belief is "*I can do it all.*"

While positive beliefs help us in supportive and beneficial ways, the negative ones do the opposite. In most cases, these beliefs arise in childhood and manifest themselves. In the depths, in secret, these thought-puppets act and directly indirectly influence our thoughts and actions. My research led to the 10 TOP limiting negative beliefs (*source: www.flowfinder.de*)

1. I am not ... enough (smart, educated, beautiful, strong, etc.).
2. It is important what others think of me.
3. I do not deserve it.
4. I am too old (young, inexperienced, etc.).
5. I could fail.
6. It takes money, luck or relationships to make money.
7. I have already tried everything.
8. I had and never have the opportunity.
9. I have no time.
10. I am a victim of my circumstances.

Only few people are actually aware of their beliefs. Years ago, it was clear to me that I wanted to get to the bottom of my beliefs to see which programs and patterns were bugging me every day. So it was up to me to find out what beliefs had concocted in me so that I could then separate the litter from the wheat.

How does that look like with you?
Do you know your beliefs? Which ones promote and which inhibit you? I like to invite you to think about it and write it down here. Remember, it is not a rating, but a consideration, scanning your mind-set. We try to get your thought pattern straight.

Think about what sentences, opinions keep coming up in your mind. What is your opinion of yourself? What do you think when you look into your reflection? What did you hear again and again as a child? Write down what you can think of:

Practi

_____

_____

?

Did you find this exercise easy? Did you feel like many people who are unaware of their beliefs? Imagine these negative beliefs clinging to you like invisible, stubborn spider monkeys. Without them, you are much better off. So go to page 165 *"Typical Negative Beliefs"* and read the listed negative beliefs. Now ask yourself: which of these beliefs keep coming up? What is your devil repeating in you all the time? You are not good enough. You are.... Not? You cannot?

_____

_____

On the next few pages, I will show you how to turn those beliefs into positives and promote those positive programs from now on. However, you have to pick out three of your negative prejudiced beliefs that you really want to get rid of. We then need these for the dissolution process.

74

Which 3 negative beliefs do you want to get rid of?

1. _____

2. _____

3. _____

Say goodbye to these negative spider monkeys, which will be soon released.

What beliefs about money do you carry around with you?
Now, it is about finding out what beliefs you have about money. After that, your material situation depends on whether you have a lot of money in your life or little.

As I began to study this topic, to my own surprise, I found that I was carrying the belief that "money is dirty" in me. In fact, I found myself washing my hands every time I wore banknotes in my hands. What do you think the love money - which is pure energy - as soon as it approached me?

Energy is attracted by energy like a magnet.

At that time, the gel energy sensed that as soon as I got it in my hands it was flushed down the water trough.

Do you recognize the gravity of this thinking? Believe me, it was unconscious. But on the contrary. Until then, I thought that I was doing everything that was beneficial, so that money was fine with me. In doing so, I did exactly the opposite with my thinking and the resulting action. After hearing about it, I addressed my mother and she explained to me, "*You swallowed coins as a baby* .... There it was! I have been a pig from an early age! I thought this thought was excellent. My mother, however, did not like this - like every mother in this situation. She did what all mothers would do. Explain to me that you did not put money into your mouth and the belief was *"money is dirty ..."*.

If you want to change your financial situation, you have to give room to your piggy bank. For this, the annoying spider monkeys have to be located and removed for the time being.

How is your attitude towards money? What do you think when you see a rich man? What thoughts come to your mind? What do you feel when you hold 1000 € bills in your hands? Choose your beliefs from the *"Negative Beliefs for Wealth, Prosperity and Money"* list (page 167).

Practice

_____

_____

Now you know what negative beliefs you carry around in terms of money. Excellent! You are a huge milestone. Remember that half the way is knowing. This step is worth a lot. Do not underestimate this!

How do you turn your negative beliefs into positives?
Now that you know which generally negative beliefs stick to you, the point is to turn them into positives. How are you going now? I ask you to pick three out of the "negative beliefs about money" list that you want to get rid of.

	Negative belief	**Positive belief**
1.	_____	_____
2.	_____	_____
3.	_____	_____

Now we turn these beliefs into positives. Take for example the belief: *"Money is dirty."* What is the positive affirmation about this? *"Money is positive energy."*

Conversion Process:

TIP

Write positive affirmation on multiple A5 cards or Post-It. Now put a labelled A5 card in your wallet, hang one of them on the bathroom mirror, stick one on your desk and put one in the car. As a result, you encounter and read the new doctrine again and again. In addition, you write this in your Happiness Journal (page 170). Once you read this new belief, you feel inward, feel your whole body absorb that positive, nourishing energy, as each of your cell attracts, fills in, and thanks you for that wonderful energy.

> **Step 1: Choose one of your negative beliefs.**
> **Step 2: Transform this belief into something positive.**
> **Step 3: Write the positive belief on a tile.**
> **Step 4: Place these cards in numerous places.**
> **Step 5: Read these cards several times a day.**
> **Step 6: Connect emotionally to this energy.**
> **Step 7: Thank you for the positive in your life.**

Complete this process of change with all your negative beliefs.

But beware: Only take one belief and pay your full attention on it. Too many at once. As a rule, less is more! I recommend that you start with a creed and apply the 21-day rule. That Within the next 21 days, you will apply this process of change to the selected belief set daily without interruption.

What happens now? You confront your thought patterns and body cells with this new sentence of your choosing. You override your hard drive (your thinking) with this new content - with the phrase "money is positive energy". That takes time. Consider for years - maybe even decades - your thinking is oriented to the opposite. Your daily reading, feeling and visualization brings you closer every day to this positive energy called money. Thanking is an essential step that expresses your doubtless confidence as a crucial last step in this process. As a result, this positive belief will prove to be a beneficial magnet for you. For more information, see the chapter "*Showing Gratitude*".

Congratulations! You have come a decisive step closer to your goal. What is your conclusion from this exercise?

_____

How do you get more money now?

Act as a rich person! Now that you've blown up your unfavourable chains of thought and let pure positive energy flow into you - open your gate, so to speak - you have to learn to act like a rich person. By that I do not mean that you walk around with money and spend it senselessly. No ... What I mean is this:

Energy is pure energy that is second to none.

Place it like a magnet in front of like-minded people. By the same principle, it works with money. Money attracts money!

What does this mean for you? There are simple methods that you can use to turn your monetary energy into something positive along with your positive beliefs. Use the following tips:

Tip 1: Always carry a 500 € or 1000 CHF bill with you

TIP

Take a € 500 note (or 1000 CHF note) and put it visibly in your wallet. You will always carry this with you. In good conscience. Every time you open your wallet, you see that bill and say inwardly, "*Money is positive energy. I attract money and I attract money. Thank you!*". So you give the message to the universe that you are a money magnet and act accordingly.

If you do not currently have a € 500 to hand, start with a € 200 check. It must be a higher sum of money for you.

78

Attention: Release yourself from the feeling of fear! Instead of fear losing your wallet, let your confidence and mindfulness dominate. Completely to Dr. Joseph Murphy's Law - What is conveyed to the unconscious as true becomes true - your carefree carrying along of this sum attracts money like a magnet.

Tip 2: Is this really necessary?

"The art is not to make money, but to keep it." This very valuable sentence was given to me by a wise and wealthy person. For many years, I carry a small card in my wallet on which the question is: "Is this really necessary?" Every time I am in a shop at the cash desk, looks at me when opening my wallet to this question. The fact is that after the critical questioning, I decide to buy 70% of the non-purchase. I spend less and have more!

TIP

You can download a template of the card on my homepage www.creativita.cc, print it and keep it in your wallet. So you profit from it by critically checking your buying behaviour.

Tip 3: Choose consciously positive company

The saying *"Show me your friends and I tell you who you are..."* says a lot. So ask yourself: What kind of friends do you have? How is your environment? Positive or more negative? Do these people lament or enjoy life? Are your friends energy-goers? Or do they radiate joy of life and happiness? Instead of surrounding yourself with passive, negative, energetic people, it is nourishing for you to surround yourself with positive, purposeful and successful people.

**Surround yourself with people
who carry these beneficial qualities!**

Let humans pull, which cause the opposite. This means that you should separate yourself from people you have been friends with for years. Remember: How much more energy is available to you from now on.

Tip 4: Put your focus on successful people

Read biographies of successful people. Who are your role models? Research about their lives. Watch videos of these people. Learn from these successful people who have become magnets of money and success and feed on it. Learn from your experiences and steps.

Tip 5: Daily work and write into your Happiness Journal

TIP

It is important to keep writing in your Happiness Journal because you're faced with goals daily and check that your compass is still heading in the right direction. This ritual will also show you the progress you make every day.

Therefore, take this time off by repeating your day and showing off your goals, achievements, reference points, and writing down as well, for which you are grateful.

Tip 6: Integrate the continuous donation to a ritual

Donations are listed in numerous surviving religious writings. The following words are found in the Bible's scriptures: *"Give, then it will be given to you. In abundant, full, abundant, overflowing measure, you will be bestowed with gifts, because according to the measure with which you measure and allocate, you will also be assigned."* (Luke chapter 6, verse 38)

Successful people like John D. Rockefeller, Marc Zuckerberg, Bill

Gates and many others have gone down in history as generous donors. Many times it is stated in this statement: "*Of course, they have the money ...*". But all three of these individuals are self-made millionaires who have integrated donations into their lives even before their monetary wealth has become a continuous act.

Like Rockefeller, who started to give 10% of his income to needy people as a child. The principle is to donate 10% of the revenue. If this seems too much for you, start with a smaller sum. What matters is that from now on you consciously give your income to the needy. Here you act on the fact:

You show with your donation that you have enough!

With this action, you identify yourself as a magnet of money and you will be given accordingly.

Tip 7: Fill you with positive affirmations
At the end of the book, I have summarized a list of "*Positive Beliefs and Affirmations for Wealth, Prosperity, and Money.*" If you say these affirmative sentences to yourself repeatedly, this will help you reprogram your unconscious thoughts and feelings.

Tip 8: Stay motivated and focused
Your environment will try to demotivate you by ridiculing your actions and refocused focus. At first, many people are sceptical and suspicious of everything new.

Attention: **This is not your energy!** Do not let yourself be demotivated! On the contrary. These statements should encourage

you in your endeavour. Do not allow a person to dissuade you from your decisions, goals, and chosen path.
It is your way! It is your decision!

These (small) excerpts of tips will support you in your everyday life and carry you in your positive energy.

This will make you a magnet for money.

Keep in mind, however, that these tips must be consistently and consistently implemented so that they can be firmly anchored in you. That is a great prerequisite and prospects, is not it?

To what extent will you heed these tips and integrate them into your everyday life? When do you start? Make a decision now and go straight into the implementation

---

Tip: In my book "Lust... for Success?" I am treating this topic more intensively. There are more tips on this topic.

The 5 main guiding principles, findings from this chapter are:

Spirituality as the essence of happiness

It is often assumed that the term *"Body, Mind and Soul"* used in our time has come down to us with its quest for perfect harmony from Asian culture. Although this is not really, true.

The spirit and soul are already present in the Bible and many other ancient antique writings. Here, the mind and soul are set in contrast to the body, which is represented as a material part of man. The soul is the conscious individuality of each, which i.a. in the intuition finds its expression. Unlike the soul, mind and body are the seat of desire and desire. These crucial three parts united as a whole harmoniously, are the key to happiness. True to the motto: *"Listen to your body, focus your mind and follow your intuition."* How does spirituality fit in?

What is it about spirituality?

Spirituality is a profound topic and enormous in its fullness. Originally, the word comes from Latin - *spiritus or spiro* - and stands for spirit and breath or I breathe. Similarly, the word psyche can be found in ancient Greek in what is spirituality.

The Internet is full of numerous explanations on this topic that in our Western world, especially by the women's world is gaining more and more importance and interest. While in Asia, people have integrated spirituality as an indispensable factor in their lives for over ten generations, and share this knowledge with their children, this is still a very young topic for us. The interest in it is revealed by the hand. Who wants to be labelled an esoteric aunt?

I have been dealing with this mystery called spirituality for a long time. Especially in my job as a tour guide, where I was able to gain experience in many different cultures, I was brought closer to this topic. Be it through encounters, talks, books or extraordinary experiences whose explanation cannot be explained with logic.

But what is spirituality? For me spirituality means to intuitively perceive things, that is, to experience them on a spiritual level. A spiritual man radiates a very special power, which inter alia u.a. composed of integrity, warmth and compassion. The so-called "rest in oneself, be in its midst" characterizes these people. No doubt about it: we feel comfortable around it and therefore like to surround ourselves with these personalities.

The question automatically comes up: how do I get these attributes and how do I become a spiritual person? I thought about it a lot, questioned it with spiritual people and devoured one book after the other on this topic. From this immense wealth of knowledge and knowledge, I have found for me the following parameters for the spiritual being, which I summarize as follows:

- **Be mindful of yourself and the environment.**
- **Listen to his heart's wisdom.**
- **Decide with common sense.**
- **Sensitize one's own mental and spiritual abilities.**
- **Develop higher consciousness.**
- **Always be in harmony with yourself and the world.**
- **Build self-confidence.**
- **Feeling connected to everyone and everything in love.**
- **Live totally in the NOW & live the current moment.**

   …last but not least…

- **Be happy!**

A big step in becoming aware of his spirituality lies in the conscious focus on the present. The NOW is the one and only. Only in here we live. Let's breathe. Yesterday has passed. The morning has not yet arrived. By contrast, the now is real and takes place right at this moment. In our fast-paced world, experiencing the moment seems to be the hardest part. Our glances are always in the past and planning is directed to the future, be it in private life or professional life.

Therefore, take this parameter - consciously living in the NOW - into your everyday life and you will see that things get a different colour and energy. You decide what you see how, and especially WHEN.

Summary Result

What is your conclusion from this? When do you start with it?

_____

Happiness is not the same happiness
Happiness is a widely used and much desired term in our language. Do you wish happiness, too?

What does luck mean exactly?
There are numerous definitions of writers and philosophers, who have dealt in detail with this question. Thus, the well-known philosopher of antiquity Aristotle says the following about the happiness to say: *"Happiness is the perfect and self-sufficient good and is the ultimate goal of human action."* His thinker colleague Plato said the following: *"Man can only be happy if the three parts of the soul, reason and will / desire are in balance."*

In today's happiness research, (Aristotle and Plato would enjoy it) basically two types of happiness are distinguished: **Happiness of life** and **Random luck!**

Where's the difference?
The **happiness of life** consists of various parameters such as love, family, friends, profession, leisure, activities and finances. These are all factors on which man can influence himself. He decides with whom he does what in his spare time.

How much money does he spend on the holiday and so on. In addition, happiness can be found in the nature and form of well-being that gives you a fantastic, great feeling of happiness. Such as, to linger in a great evening with his friends or when your child smiles at you. Duden defines happiness as follows: *"Fulfilment and happiness in one's own private life"*.

In the case of random luck - as the name implies - chance decides whether one is lucky or not. Is that really so? Who believes in chance, determination and destiny? The state is making millions by extolling with lush lottery money.

Fact is: Random luck cannot be controlled. However, the attitude to the situation. There are also the options of being welcome and open or closed and dismissive. Those who act in a closed manner accept random luck as a disruption - true to the motto: "*Do not challenge your luck.*" Individuals who are more open to random luck see opportunities and challenges in them. According to the principle: **Everyone is the architect of his own fortune!**

Happiness determines our lives and we all want to have as much as possible of it. Here are some tips for you:

• **Give luck to your life a chance**
Be open to new ideas and adopt a courageous, curious and positive attitude. Life is rich in opportunities!

• **Get rid of social norms**
Away with it ... Separate yourself from norms that hang like fetters on you. You want to do something new (job, etc.)? Start today! It is your life. You decide the content.

• **Do not search for love**
Do not waste time waiting for Mr Right to knock on you. Enjoy life with friends and yourself. Mr. Right will make you more attractive when you are bursting with happiness!

• **Laugh about yourself**
The French comedian, Louis de Funès, put it in a nutshell: "*Laughter is the same to the soul as oxygen to the lungs*". The ability to laugh at your own mistakes and mishaps is precious and makes you easy. Do not take yourself so seriously, but with humour. Now you are laughing at yourself most heartily ... OK?

• **Enjoy the moment!**

We humans are very much inclined to stay in the past or in the future. In doing so, we walk with our thoughts like a pendulum between yesterday and tomorrow without interruption. For our well-being, it is so much more valuable to fully experience here and now. Practice living the moment in it. This will make you u.a. the colours are more intense, the wind more powerful and the sun more radiant. In short: experience life much better! Therefore, pay attention to it:

Enjoy the moment before it becomes a memory.

It is completely in your hands as you accept happiness. People, who are at peace with themselves and thereby experience the ability of the feeling of happiness with all their senses, are great role models!

What do you take with it? What is your conclusion?

_____

Summary Result

You are what you think...

Have you heard of them? **The laws of life...**

I know that law is a very strict word, and at once leaves a trace of defiance. However, laws are in place that the meaningfulness is carved in stone and thus unshakable. This is completely confirmed by the laws of life. The laws of life are clear parameters that everything in and around us revolves around. We are in daily contact with these numerous laws of life. However, we rarely realize it. One of the laws of life and arguably the most important law of the universe is this:

!

Law of cause and effect

This law of "*cause and effect*" is also known as "*Law of attraction*", "*Karma law*" and "*Causality law*".

What does this law say? It says that in the universe, nothing happens by accident, but everything has a recognizable cause. Every cause follows an effect. Synonymous: Every effect arises from a cause! In

88

plain English this means that in the way we do something, we will get it back! If we want to change the effect, we have to change the cause. The following proverbs come to my mind:

As you call into the forest, it resounds!
What you sow, you harvest!

The same system automatically occurs when you get up in the morning with the famous "false foot" and how a zombie swoons through the day. Everything looks grey on you, the people around you annoy you. As your day gets worse for you and more and more grey clouds form, you wonder what is going on. But when you start the day with a laugh and a grateful, happy feeling, embracing the world for joy, you will be perceived as a sunshine by the people. Joy and goodwill meet you.

What happened?
You decide how your day goes. If you are in a bad mood, you shout into the forest with your posture, aura, words and thoughts, how badly your day will be perceived by you. Likewise, your environment will reflect this to you. Grey and in a bad mood.

You get this back. On the other hand, when you live full of joy, nourishing thoughts, and benevolent positive words, this is reflected in your life, environment, work, family, and friends.

Is not that wonderful? The law of cause and effect is always in use and is determined by you all alone in which direction it turns. This is just one of many laws of life. On my website you will be able to read more about the laws of life.

Be honest with yourself. How do you use the law of cause & effect? Are you more in grey, dreary climes or are you the true colourful creative artist of your life? What do you learn from this for you?

Summary
Result
_____

Intuition, gut feeling & the sixth sense

Intuition, also known as gut feeling and sixth sense, is found intuitively in the original Latin word *intuitio*, which stands for immediate intuition, or closer look. In general, inputs, sensations and thoughts are understood that come about without thinking and have their origin in the subconscious. These intuitive ideas, gut feelings, flashes of thought cannot be explained rationally.

I personally see intuition as the intriguing ability to listen deeply, to feel, to perceive and, without explicit contexts, to be able to immediately call a decision that then proves to be correct in its implementation.

Do you know that we women use intuition much more often and rely on it more often than our male colleague relies? Very useful to care for and understand our sensitive multi-faceted world. We let ourselves be guided by our gut feeling, inner voice or sixth sense. Can in the truest sense of the word smell and recognize danger when we are lied to by the partner. How does this work? An invisible antenna lets women receive many invisible things. A great thing! Better than the mind and spirit? Albert Einstein answers as follows: *"Intuition is a divine gift. The thinking mind a faithful servant. It is paradoxical that today we have begun to worship the servant and profane the divine gift. "*

Of course, men also carry this ability in themselves. However, it can be said that the women have deeply rooted and developed this talent over the millennia in their sensation. From birth, we were born of this ability and forgotten in our world because of too little attention.

Intuition constantly sends messages to us. We are constantly confronted with it. The question is whether we are on reception or not. For example, if a good friend contacts you and you have thought of him a moment or you're worried about a friend, because you intuitively feel she's not well. In the case of personal questioning, this turns out to be correct.

Intuition is an outstanding radar device that is in direct contact with your soul. Intuition is a sophisticated, battery-free transmitter that we always carry with us. Intuition is like a personalized answer to your questions. Use it!

You carry that true gift in yourself. It is a wonderful, extraordinary gift to train. It is the heritage of all our ancestors, women to thank, who have perfected this knowledge, this ability & gave us. Thank you!

Now it is entirely up to you how you handle this capability with this receiver. How did you use your intuition so far? Are you in direct daily rapport with it? How often do you go back to that?

_____

_____

TIP To train the perception of your intuition and thus easier to get answers to your questions; go into it now, when it comes to a decision. Ask for your inner response to your acute question, for a sign. Be careful which thoughts, feelings and sensations come over you. You cannot score at this moment. It is best to write down everything that comes to your mind.

In my daily happiness journal, I also devote myself to my intuition by expressing my thanks for advice or asking questions in writing. Within a few days, I usually have answers that present as a gut feeling, as lightning thoughts or as a sign in nature.

Of course, it only works if the mindfulness and the consciousness are on reception. Therefore, always be alert, present and in the here and now! There are lying in your answers.

_____

Rendezvous with your I

If you meet a person and find him likable, you want to know more about this person. How are you proceeding? By spending time with him, asking questions, listening to his stories, watching him. From the wealth of information, you make your picture about this person. In the same way, this works with you. With your I/ME!

The only difference is that you have been traveling with yourself for some time. You mean to know your I/ME know you well, to know them inside out and actually believe that your I have nothing more to tell you. Exactly the opposite of the case!

You have a lot to tell yourself. Such as new insights you have collected, unspoken desires, deeply hidden ideas that are seeking your attention.

That is, it is time for you to take time for your I/ME, to re-enter, to re-examine, and to learn to accept again. How do you do this best? Very easily! You take your time by arranging rendezvous times for your meeting with your I/ME. Clearly scheduled and then carry out. Alone. Moreover, I mean all alone.

That may sound funny and may feel that way. Nevertheless, dare this step. What do you have to lose? Some time. What you will gain by this is worth much more than you can currently imagine.

Now think about how much time daily you take for yourself? I do not mean the daily toilet, but the time in which you deal with yourself. For example, are you already taking the time for your Têtê-a-Têtê?

Practice

The Têtê-a-Têtê Time is a very good start to engage with yourself and re-encounter your I/ME. As you already know, when you write in your lucky journal, you are concerned with recognizing & writing down the goals, the things you are thankful for, the successes of the day. In the rendezvous with your I/ME, you invest time by doing things after your inner I aspire and desire inwardly. You kind of stroke your I/ME with activities that fill your cells with energy. That gives enormous joy of life.

In order to do that you have to know in advance which favourite activities you have not taken any time for. Maybe a parachute jump or the visit of your favourite city Paris? Alternatively, just lying relaxed on a meadow that stretch limbs and stare into the sky. Think about it & capture your thoughts. Just write down what comes to your mind.

_____

_____

What thoughts have you encountered? Even surprised? Women tend to serve others and usually forget themselves. Man is a lot happier, happier and more productive when doing things that are fun for him / her. So it is time for you to start actively doing those activities your soul craves.

Be aware of times in your week planning for your rendezvous with your I. Request this time! Because you are most important to yourself. Coordinate your duties and duties by asking your loved ones for help. It actually starts with your decision to take your time for yourself. Thus…

When will your first Rendezvous with yourself take place? **Ruling**
What are you planning to do?

_____

Start writing down your thoughts now. Let them bubble, flow and record them. Thoughts wander and are like drops in a raging river. Keep a notebook and pen ready so that you can always hold on to these thoughts straight away.

Wellness & Spa for 1

Even the ancient Romans and the Ottoman people knew how to use the energy sources of wellness and spa (*sanus per aquam*, which means health through water). It was not only about the physical cleansing, but the mental purification was also an important factor.

Wellnessen is a trend that is more popular than ever as a weekend getaway. Especially couples use this luxury to relax and pamper themselves. Likewise, there are a variety of girlfriends offers in which ladies can devote themselves together to their beauty and body.

TIP

My suggestion to you:
Wellness & Spa for 1! Exactly, only you with your I allow yourself a break from your environment, home, family. That is perfectly legitimate and nothing speaks against it as long as you're worth it.

Wellness & Spa for 1 time is a tremendously valuable and nourishing time for you as a person, but especially for you as a woman. For your body and soul. Taking care of your own beautiful, beautifully functioning body, having it pampered with massages means getting to know your body anew. Likewise to learn to re-appreciate. So ask yourself now spontaneously:

On a scale of 1 to 10: How do you love your body? _____

Practic

Studies show that most women are dissatisfied with their bodies. They find the nose is too big, too thick, the legs too clumsy and the arms too wobbly. Be assured:

Your body is perfect and beautiful!

It depends entirely on your thinking about how you take charge of your body. If you lovingly and lovingly accept your body with respect and gratitude, you will realize how much your attitude to your own body changes. As soon as you feel in your body, it is transferred to the outside.

No matter if, you have clothes size 36 or 44 now. The only thing that matters is HOW you feel with your body.

Wellness & Spa for 1 is a wonderful opportunity for you to take the time, space and freedom to resonate with your body. Talk to him. Caress him. Care for him. Spoil him! Very important: Thank you with him. It is not self-evident that our legs bring us from A to B. Many people are not granted this privilege. What would these sufferers do for healthy legs?

I treat myself to this break for years in which I spoil my body and let my soul dangle. What valuable knowledge and experiences I was allowed to take from it so far. When I took this time for the first time and I sat alone in the hotel dining room at my table, met many questioning, surprised and compassionate looks. However, I also noticed wistful looks in some women's eyes.

Therefore, treat yourself to this time-out. Start by treating yourself to a 1-day spa near you. Book a nice aroma oil massage and let yourself be carried away by the pleasure of enjoying it. This is worth your while as a thoroughbred woman!

What does being a woman mean completely?
An interesting and important question at the same time. Are there any criteria, standards and guidelines that today's woman can follow? Alternatively, is the perception, the perception of the woman being individually different?

My research has shown me one thing clearly: There is no clear definition for it! For every woman, being a woman means something different. Individually different women understand this context personally.

I interviewed many women from different cultures and collected some of their feedback on the question, "**What does it mean for you to be a pure woman?**":

- To live the legacy of my female ancestors.
- Use the freedom to do what I prefer.
- To live the strength and the weakness at the same time.
- To give human lives.
- To live different roles (daughter, mother, wife etc.)
- To live the creative power completely.
- To bring out the mystery in me.
- To love me 100% with all my mistakes and blemishes.
- Strong as a lion and as gentle as a lamb at the same time.
- To give away infinite, powerful love.
- To discover and live the very own power in me.
- Feeling as comfortable in my body as I am.
- To live my female and male side in synergies.

All statements are individual considerations and the result is therefore quite different. Where they are in the same: There is neither right nor wrong. Now the crucial question: What does being a woman mean to you?

_____

_____

How easy was this exercise for you? It may well be that initially it is difficult for you to answer this question. That is fine. Think about this question in peace. Take notes and set the time until you want to define your clear and unambiguous meaning for you.

Ask yourself what factors you use to judge your personal being as a woman. What criteria do you use? These are your very personal criteria. That is why there is no right or wrong. These are to be put on paper for you, so that they are tangible and, above all, visible.

_____

_____

In addition, it is legitimate for you to change your answer over time.

Nothing is as constant as change. You as a human being are constantly in the process of change, of change. So do not be too strict with yourself and grant yourself the right to change your meaning for you, if you think so. What is your conclusion from this?

_____

_____

How much pure woman-being do you live?

Now that you have defined for yourself, what it means for you to be a woman, I ask you: How much womanhood do you really live out? Which grade from 1 to 10 do you give yourself? Be quite critical and question you: _____

I confess, when I asked myself this question for the first time at the age of 32, I got a bad 4. The question that I asked myself was: Which criteria and how much womanhood did I really live according to my own best knowledge and conscience?

I realized that I derived my opinion about how much woman I believed to be from the resonance of the male world. Since I was considered sexy by the male world, I felt exactly that, sexy and sought after. This realization was sobering.

I actually had a lot of catching up to do! I simply did not know what parameters I should weigh and evaluate my being a woman. However, I knew that it was not on the body size, form nor in the way the men looked. The more I thought, researched, and dealt with it, the more obvious it became. The answer is clear and unambiguous:

The key is inside each person!

Thus, I began to rediscover myself and pure-being-woman. I went on a research trip, so to speak, ignoring the reactions & opinions of my outside world, externally, which, I must confess, was not easy at first.

Everything starts with knowing! With the neutral determination, clarification, recognition. To get from A to B it is important to know where the respective locations are. Because only then is it clear how much it takes to get from A to B. Therefore do not hold back.

How much womanhood will you live in the future? Do you feel how you are already nourished by this decision? Do you realize what a wonderful gift it is to be a woman?

Unleash your thoroughbred woman in you

Women have enormous abilities & talents in them. Together, these give a bundle of immeasurable energy, endless love & power to move the mountains! A mother who tries to save her child from an awkward situation leaves untold forces free to do so! All women carry in themselves this incredible energy of a thoroughbred woman!

Recognizing this is the key to unleashing your full-blooded wife in you. You are a wonderful creature! Pure love! A powerful energy stream, a volcano of passion! You are a thoroughbred woman! Get rid of your deadlocked opinions by letting your inside speak and act. You are in the now. Yesterday has passed and tomorrow is far away. Your actions today decide what will happen tomorrow.

We have no influence on the past,
decide our tomorrow through our action today.

How long do you want to leave your well-guarded treasure of passion buried deep in the dark in your heart? How long do you want to deny your own calls for freedom?

Be the woman to whom you were born! Be the warrior who screams for freedom in you! Your thoroughbred wife Gene is the trickster who has shown you what you have several times in the past. What is inside you. In doing so, you perceived this power as exciting and dangerous at the same time.

Accept this power, energy, passion after pure life. You carry them deep in your cells since you were born. As a thank you to all our ancestors, you are carrying your heritage.

Now when you look in the mirror, recognize this fighter, warrior, the woman that you are.

Purebred woman pure!

Make the decision no longer to hide this part of your wife. Instead, you give her room, the stage, the spotlight. What do you give her?

The 5 main guiding principles, findings from this chapter are:

Your body is your home !

Your body is a marvel! A fantastic, sophisticated, unique work that Mother Nature created to perfection and cannot duplicate a computer in this form. Let's take a closer look at your extraordinary body:

Stupendous facts about your body

Your body is made out of 60-80% water, depending on your age. Your skeleton is about 12% of your body weight and consists of 300 bones / cartilage & 100 joints. Amazing! As a baby, you still had 350 bones, some of them growing together. Your skin is with a surface of 1 ½ to 2 square meters your largest sensory organ and a very delicate. Of your 656 muscles, the masticatory muscle is the strongest.

That in itself is very impressive!
Did you know that your gut has a total length of 5.5 - 7.5 meters? Or that the total length of your nerve cords in the body is as much as 780,000 kilometres? This is actually once back to the moon. What a route! In addition, you lose over 3 kilograms of skin cells every year. This means that your skin is completely renewed once a month. Your stomach acid is so aggressive that it can dissolve razorblades. Luckily, there is your stomach wall which prevents damage of this kind. Your sneeze has the speed of 160 km / h, while your heart beats about 33 million times a year.

In addition, the women's body offers more taste-nerves than men, according to studies. Women can thus judge within a wine degustation better! Over 8000 nerve endings supply the clitoris. That is twice as much as the glans penis. (*source: www.watson.com*). What does all this tell us? Your body is a true masterpiece!

Your body is a true treasure

Have you ever considered what treasure you have with your body? What extraordinary tool was given to experience your life with the senses of smelling, feeling, tasting, hearing and seeing?

In fact, your body is effectively the only thing that you have effectively. If you are allow calling a home your own, it is theoretically your property. Logical! Finally, your name will appear in the documents provided. The difference to your body is a decider! While you cannot carry your house around with you, you are constantly doing this with your body 24 hours a day, 364 days a year.

The fact is, most people are unaware of this treasure and wonder. They take their bodies for granted and see no reason to humbly thank them daily for this impeccable, beautiful body. On the contrary, for the most part, only one thing is done about this outstanding body, which works with all its wonderful functions and systems in the best possible synergy: it is pulled through the shortage, criticized!

What do you think of when you hear the word treasure? A crowded box of gold coins? A room full of gold bars? To your heart leaf? For the most part, we humans in the Western world associate the term treasure with material goods such as money, wealth, jewellery, gold bars, etc.

Strictly speaking, it is from the consideration - what really counts - only your own body is your true treasure. Your body, which can feel and transport the harmonious well-being, the feeling of happiness and the experience of pure love! Neither a gold bullion nor the largest ring with the thickest diamond can replace these emotions.

It is only the confrontation with illness and physical disabilities that is experienced in observation or on one's own body, which allows people to realize how important and valuable a healthy and perfectly functioning body is in itself. Do you recognize your body as a treasure?

You are the treasurer of your body. You only have one body and this one is unique, a diamond. He is an indispensable part of you and therefore very special. That is fact and irrefutable.

Do you feel good with your body?

On the other hand, another question is how happy you are with your body, figure, your outward appearance, happiness. On a scale of 1 to 10, which grade do you give yourself? _____ Please ask yourself, what do you like about your body?

_____

_____

Practice

How did you feel about this question? At first, only your stains came to mind? The bacon rolls, cellulite and wrinkles. We humans tend to deal primarily with the stigma rather than focus on the positive. It is up to you how you think about yourself.

According to a survey, 90% of women are dissatisfied with their bodies. A shockingly high and worrying number! Why is that? Is it because women compare too much with perfectly styled celebrities and models?
The broadcast of the 13th season of the reality show "*Germanys Next Topmodell*" in May 2018 shows the uninterrupted interest in the models. The specifications of the modelling industry are extremely strict. Women use methods that endanger their health to reach the size of 32/34 and end in the hamster wheel of bulimia or anorexia.

The model, which is smiling from the colourful billboards, displays a body that has nothing to do with reality anymore. Graphical software programs provide tighter parts, longer legs, flawless skin, a narrower face or a longer neck with just a few mouse clicks. Today's poster women are a software product of yesteryear and lastingly adversely affect girls, teenagers and women.

In the documentary "*Embrace - you are beautiful*" Taryn Brumfitt deals with the beauty ideal of women in the Western world.

TIP

Here, the Australian tells very authentically about her personal involvement with her character, her dissatisfaction among them and tries to identify the causes in the film. The extent to which this topic concerns women all over the world is shown by the fact that this film landed on the first evening (May 2017) in the German cinemas on number 1 of the charts. The hitherto most successful event ever. (*source: www.wikipedia.de*)

"*Embrace - you are beautiful*" is a remarkable movie that every woman should watch. Why? Since this film - as *Filmstarts.de* stated - is a committed plea against the slimming & youth delusion of society and stands for the diversity of female beauty! In the film, the author explains how her life has completely changed due to the valuable insight "*What brings you a beautiful body when you are not happy?*. The aim of the film is to make women aware of a changed perception of the woman's body and thereby make her happier.

How can you promote your awareness and positive perception of your body in the long term? Actively engaging yourself with the following tips will help you a lot in the positive perception of yourself:

• **Get rid of your negative opinion about you & your character!**
The more positive you are with yourself, the more positive you are with your appearance. By doing so, you promote your healthy body self-awareness and access to yourself.

• **Go lovingly with you!**
Overload yourself with love. Smile your reflection daily heartily. Choose something new every day (a thing, activity, etc.) with which you make yourself happy.

• **Be your best friend!**
Take care of yourself as you accept your best friend. No ifs and buts. You are perfect as you are!

• **Write yourself loving messages!**

... I agree! Leave messages in your calendar or put small pieces of paper in your wallet on which says, "You're great!", "As you are, you're perfect!", "You're beautiful," "You have the perfect body, figure!", "I love you!"

• **Laugh a lot and about yourself!**

"A day without laughter is a lost day." Laugh a lot every day, hearty and unrestrained! Laugh at yourself! About your mistakes, blemishes, weaknesses. The more you put your foot down, the less pressure, expectation, and more respect you have for yourself.

You are perfect the way you are.

Health is the biggest wealth

The above wise quote brings it to the point. What does wealth mean when health is struck? When disease dominates everyday life, the importance of health becomes clearer to the person concerned. All money in the world has no value if illness dominates the body. *"Take care of your body. He's the only place you have to live!"*

No luxurious mansion or beach house can replace your human body. It is important to nurture and nurture your only body with great care. The effort to keep your health intact should be focused on the harmonious union of your body, mind and soul. These are inevitably linked.

What are you doing to keep your body, mind and soul healthy?

Body: _____

Mind: _____ Practice

Soul: _____

Are you satisfied with your answers? Do you also realize the potential to work more actively on your health?

Let's take a quick look at how you can balance this constellation. Your unique body can be kept in good condition with sufficient sleep, a well-balanced diet and lots of exercise and exercise. Sport does not only make you physically fit, it also has a positive effect on your mental health, your self-confidence and your general body image. In order to stay mentally fit it is therefore advisable to read a lot, to undergo regular cognitive training (such as playing a musical instrument) and brain jogging.

TIP

Regular social interactions are good, effective and just good. To keep your mind in balance, the following general manipulations are helpful:

- Focus your attention on the present - the now.
- Think positive! Everything has its good side and reasons.
- Be unique and special.
- Practice your composure (inter alia through meditation).
- Do not discount other people! Learn from them.
- ... laugh heartily every day!

Teresa of Avila summed it up as follows: *"Treat your body well so that the soul feels like living in it."*

What consequence do you draw from this for you?

Summary Result

_____

Clothes make people...

This saying comes from the poet Gottfried Keller. What it means is that the opinion - that is, the first impression - about a person of his clothing is determined in advance.

Imagine the following scenario: A man in dirty, sloppy clothes staggers on a pedestrian precinct and then falls over. The same happens to the same man only this time he wears a flawless suit. What do you think? Which outfit evokes help actions faster?

106

Bingo: The man, dressed in a suit, is immediately helped by several people, while the same man is slowly relieved of his clothes in storage-costumes after a few minutes.

Why is that? In the first impression, which is established within a few seconds, the person is very influenced by the external appearance. Albeit unconsciously!

Fact is: In our society, the clothes have a very high priority. The fashion industry lays the new trend twice a year. This includes the clothing style, accessories and the hairstyle style, which then dominates the season. An incredible business! Man and woman of the world hold in the best manner to these specifications and buy what is considered beautiful and current. After all, they want to be modern and trendy. Likewise, the Knigge (*which relies on the book "Dealing with Man", published by Adolph Freiheit Knigge in 1788*) steers his own and also reinforces people's moral concept.

What does this mean for you as a thoroughbred woman? Are there any rules you should follow? Do you have to squeeze yourself in high heels as a thoroughbred woman? Does today's thoroughbred woman only wear tight, figure-hugging dresses? How do you think a thoroughbred woman dresses?

_____

Practice

_____

From my point of view, there is only one thing to say:

**The more authentically you dress,
the more you will feel like a thoroughbred woman!**

What does that mean? If you like high heels with sheath dress then do that! Do you prefer a sportier style ... Go for it! It is important that you give expression to your perfect style. In clothes in which you feel comfortable, you move harmoniously, united. In short: Authentic!

Do you have a style? Are you aware of your own style? In what clothes do you feel comfortable? Female? Authentic?

_____

_____

The more you are aware of your own style the better you live it out. No matter what other people say. It is important that you feel comfortable in it. True to the motto: **Your clothes are your expression of yourself!**

Sport is not murder but life

People who are more likely to be divided into their own sports activities like to use the saying Sport is murder. The opposite is the case!

Any form of physical activity is good for our body, mind and soul. Our body is not made to sit or lie on the couch all day. Instead, he needs exercise, fresh air, physical activity that raises the pulse. Otherwise he becomes lethargic, lazy and lax. Jogging not only improves your condition and strengthens your muscles, but also gives the mind space, removes everyday stress, gets rid of intellectual legacy and at the same time thrive new ideas.

Numerous studies show that sports activities make people happy because endorphins, dopamine and serotonin are released. This is sometimes a reason to integrate sports into your everyday life. But there are other reasons:

1. Burns Fat: Speaks entirely for yourself!
2. Counteracts high blood pressure: That is always good!
3. Makes Muscle Grow: Well please ... Best!
4. Strengthens cardiovascular system: Keeps you healthy!
5. Make happy: Well, That is definitely the best thing about it!

In short: Whoever moves, trains his body and mind!

Not only do you gain muscle, but also boost your self-confidence, strengthen your composure and let u.a. increase your thinking power. Clearly good reasons for sports and physical activity.

How do you feel about the sport? Is physical activity an indispensable part of your everyday life? Which physical activities are part of your life?

_____

_____

What did the questions tell you? Are you satisfied with the result? Or do you realize that you could do more activities in your life? If yes, which?

Summary Result

_____

There are a variety of sports to choose from, depending on your preference and the season. And every year new sporting inventions are added. Wikipedia has listed well over 200 sports. Where to start? Is the agony of choice?

TIP

No. It does not matter which sport you actively take up and operate in your life. It is important that you move consciously and continuously, so that your body and mind remain fit and that makes you feel happy and comfortable.

Because the fitter you feel,
the more pleasure and joy
has your soul to stay in your body!

Apropos: There is a physical activity that shoots your heart rate 100% and undoubtedly leads your body, mind and soul into ecstasy! You wonder what exactly I mean? The next chapter reveals more ..

The 5 main guiding principles, findings from this chapter are:

Do you have sexual fulfilment...

Satisfied sexuality is an important milestone in our lives. Fulfilled sexuality supports the happy & harmonious life and supports your ICH. The question that arises is whether you are aware of it and live it out? Or do you rather not stand by it and thus feel a big gap in your life?

Sex in Society

Many times, I hear the claim that in this century we are very open about sexuality. I smile, for I remember the ancient Romans and, of course, the Greeks, who lived out their sexual appetites in all directions and, above all, captured them figuratively. Thus, we know very well that men practiced sex with peers just as openly while being married and fathers at the same time. Women did the same and it was not discarded at all, but was fully in vogue and integrated into everyday life. The ancient Romans loved exuberant, exuberant festivals, and everything was allowed. We can say that, from the point of view of the Western world, swinger club, group sex and bisexuality started in the ranks of Roman and Greek walls.

> Throughout, there are further traces of a completely open uncomplicated and value-free exercise of sexuality in other cultures and eras again.

In our time, the twenty-first century, we are quite open to sexuality in Western society. Nobody would have thought a few years ago that a homosexual in noble women's clothing with a wild dark mane and an unmistakable beard would win the Eurovision Song Contest 2016. A huge breakthrough for the gay scene. Despite critical opinions, this decision was celebrated in many countries.

Likewise, the bureaucracy is showing more and more openness and concessions by allowing peer-to-peer marriage to become an official marriage (*Netherlands since 2000, Germany since 01/01/2017, Austria from 01/01/2019)*, pushing the current registered partnership into the corner. This development is quite pleasing. Similarly, the possibility that a gay couple can adopt children shows how open our society has evolved in this direction. This would have been unimaginable decades ago.

That this open attitude is not supported by every human being and culture is not incomprehensible. Development takes time. As the word development already implies, unwinding focuses on unravelling old patterns from their basic ideas, so that space and space for new thoughts can be created. This requires time and patience of the viewer. However, it can be said that in this respect we are on the trail of our Greek and Italian ancestors.

Monogamy and polygamy
In various cultures, polygamy is a firmly implemented and lived social pattern that is not shaken. In our societies, on the other hand, monogamy has become the only and true way of life, while polygamy is considered frowned upon and selfish. So is it a surprise that many men want that? Away from monogamy and polygamy.

Of 10 men surveyed, whether they would like to have sex with several women at the same time, seven have answered in the affirmative. There the ego speaks as the impeller. Men always want to prove their ego. This is not judgmental, but a natural evolution of manhood. The hunting instinct for millennia deep in itself, it is precisely the women conquests that serve the man as trophies for his ego.

To live this out in the form of a polygamy form of relationship is beguiling in so far as this form sends out a clear message to the outside: *"I am a great, irresistible stallion."*

How does this the world of women?
Well, there is the one group who totally consider this thought

112

reprehensible and repugnant. It absolutely contradicts their basic idea of harmonious partnership with the one, with their Mr. Right. Imagining that her petal also enters into a relationship with another or even more women - whether on an emotional or physical level - is an absolute taboo. Why? They themselves have opted for this way of life. Absolute loyalty and dedication for the one and only. Point.

Then there is the other women's group. The one who is attracted to the idea of having a physical relationship with several men at the same time. Very few ladies really live up to these secret wishes. If they do, then secretly without the knowledge of friends and their environment.

But wait: Is this really so reprehensible? For the woman after all. Because it still dominates an old-established pattern of the social form and opinion. While the man in a lively relationship with several women is smiled by society smiling as macho, the woman is just the opposite, a hussy. Is it therefore because women behave more restrained because they do not want to surrender to the usual forms of society and the reprehensible opinions? It is in the nature of women that they are intent on harmony. Women are the peacemakers in the family and environment with their tremendous skills of empathy. The tendency is to overshadow their own needs and preferences.

Hand on heart: Did you ever wish that? Imagined how it would be if you could live out your sexual desires with different man?

Oh you mean, that is reprehensible? That is not possible? Where would we get there? Keep in mind that this workbook is yours and you should therefore honestly answer this question.
There is nothing wrong with it, if you cherish cravings of this kind. A multitude of women cherish these secret desires, but do not live them out. The reasons are complex.

It is important for you to understand your wishes and to decide whether you want to live them out or not. Being honest with yourself is a prerequisite, because it is all about the most important thing in your life: your life!

What is your conclusion? What did you learn for yourself?

_____

Cheating is a decision...

I am always amazed how many couples are cheating. Of course, the "better half" knows nothing of this snack in foreign climes. What is invisible and unimaginable to the person concerned is an open book for mindful observers. In some cases, both main actors simultaneously use each other differently without being aware of each other.

It clearly shows that these people are not happy in their own relationship, that they do not feel fulfilled. Instead of facing these problems, this gap is filled by the relationship with another person. They believe to find in the stranger, the new one the happiness that was lost in one's own relationship. The fact that this makes the situation a lot more complicated, recognize the affected only when it is already too late. In addition, in the secrecy of strangers in the midst of mysterious and forbidden, which promotes the kick and pushes adrenaline. An emotional tightrope act for all actors.

Why is? To the feeling of happiness? To feel loved and desired? Is strangulation the solution? What begins as a harmless flirtation that flatters the ego can end in cheating. The person has to face the following consequences sooner or later. This prescribes the law of cause and effect inevitably. Only at what price?

What does this behaviour say? That the couple should part, before they make out with others? Can it be that monogamy as a way of life is not the ideal form of partnership for that person? Only one person can answer this critical question for himself.

114

It is important how you feel about yourself. Do you have any fantasies that you have not lived through? You have not shared with your partner yet? Do you have secret desires that you would like to experience with your partner or others? Be open to yourself and write down your thoughts.

Which are these? Remember this is your workbook to which you can confide everything. What matters is only your personal view.

_____

_____

What is your conclusion? What did you learn for yourself?

_____

Enlightenment ... "*What I always wanted to know...*"
The love of enlightenment is an issue in itself. Then and still today. I belong to the generation that grew up with the well-known and popular youth magazine "Bravo" and was educated. There was Dr. Summer, which tackled all the teenage issues of puberty, physical development, first sex and general sex issues. Instead of just writing a quick e-mail, the eager for answer young people took the trouble and wrote a letter. Yes, exactly one letter! These were published anonymously under the heading "What I always wanted to know". Thousands of young people then consumed and nourished it. This may seem strange today, but at the time there were not many books and resources that could have been accessed. Unless an adult was asked about it, which was rather rare.

Our embarrassed parents were completely overwhelmed with the education work. As post-war children, they themselves did not benefit from an open education, because far different priorities were on the agenda. I remember that sex education was in our 4th grade primary school curriculum. Our brave and motivated teacher made

115

the greatest effort to lead us on the path of enlightenment, with a high red face. However, when he projected the images of female and male genitalia on the wall with the beamer in large format, we were giggling children's gang out of whack and tape. That was it! This proved to be the only attempt. After that, the subject of sex education was removed from the class schedule.

Thus, Dr. med. Sommers written statements & verbal explanations, which we caught up with from the older adolescents, are very popular.

Today - it is assumed - everything is better. The Internet offers an enormous amount of knowledge that the searcher can easily access with a few mouse clicks. Likewise, in many schools, sex education as a fixed subject in the curriculum is very popular. Thus, the children and young people are well served with knowledge from all sides. However, studies show that children are still very ignorant today. This is also evidenced by the high birth rates of offspring born by children between the ages of 13 and 17. For example, believe Teenagers that introduced sperm during a bath cannot lead to a pregnancy.

TIP

Thus it can be said: It is up to each parent to educate their children to the best of their knowledge and to ensure that their child knows what it is about, what is important, how to protect against AIDS and venereal diseases and how it can lead to pregnancy.

Of course, this assumes that the parents themselves know what works. Women in particular should be able to explain out of the box how our menstrual cycle works and how our sexual organs work, because they are an important and indispensable part of ourselves.

If you realize that, you do not know exactly what is where and need to research the internet to explain your monthly cycle, be reassured. There you are not alone. Many women feel that way. Take remedial action by making yourself smart. For this I have at the end of the book a statement of the genitalia of women and men (cannot hurt) installed and also added an explanation of the menstrual cycle, which gives you a good insight into the wonder world of women's body.

In fact, the female body is a true treasure that truly has the ability to create a new human in its lap. No machine, no computer and no man are capable! This is reserved solely for women. Women are Picassos and Leonardo da Vinci's, because they create true human works of art. That is something to keep in mind.

TIP

Please do not disturb…
The basic requirement for a fulfilled sexuality is the exploration of one's own body. Of course, this includes self-satisfaction! Only when you know yourself, you can communicate to the outside what you like. No matter what age you are, it is about taking your time and the leisure to explore yourself and your body. It is wonderful to do this because your body is a land of plenty of emotions just waiting to be discovered and explored by yourself.

• Take your time
This journey of discovery takes time. Treat yourself to these. Plan this intimate time several times a week for you.

• Be smart
It is helpful if you know your own body. You should know how sexual arousal works in women. See tip on the back.

• Choose a quiet and private place
To really let you go, you need a quiet, private place to retire. It is useful to be able to lock the door.

• Follow your instincts
Do not shame on your body. This one, with all its wonderful sensations, has been made to use the wonders of the feelings for you. Thus, let yourself completely on your sense and discover you completely without shame.

• **Toiletries for pampering**
Use the wide variety of care products such as oil. These feel wonderful and smell fantastic. This also animates your sense of smell and increases your sensual sensitivity.

• **Try new practices**
You want to try new sex practices? Do not you dare? You want to experiment, but do not know where? There are varieties of different sexual practices, such as swingers club, sex with peers, threesomes, group sex, bondage, etc. The Internet opens the door to unite with like-minded people. It has never been so easy to find out what happens when and where your preference. It is only up to you to find out and use this information for yourself.

> **Attention:** Do not forget your sound mind. Inquire in detail about the establishment and individuals before venturing into this foreign realm. Your lust must not distract you from your clear mind. Then the enjoyment and pleasure are safe too!

• **Sex toys**
Should it be a sex toy? Why not? Let yourself be inspired by the variety of possibilities, for example by going to a Beate Uhse store. The internet also offers a variety of great choices that you can access within a few mouse clicks. Try out!

• **To let yourself fall**
Indispensable in the fulfilled sexuality is the dropping. Leave your inhibition behind and trust your body, who knows what he wants. Let go of concerns or feelings of shame. By simply giving free rein to your feelings, desires, and lust, you will rediscover your body.

The human body, with all its thousands of cells, is a wonderful construct of sensations and feelings that will lead to a great sea of emotions in active movement.

Just try it!

What sexual experiences do you bring with you?

Each person is at a different point in terms of sexual experience. While some have collected all their sexual experiences with their sandbox love, others have explored their experiences in many different realms. It is not important with how many partners you have brought your body to the ectasias, but what you have taken from it.

Many women have confirmed to me that they have experienced one-night-stands as probably the most uncomplicated form of relationship, as long as they are confined to a purely physical level.

The reason is obvious: Both parties know what it is all about: Sex and fun! Without ifs and buts, without wondering what the next day is, without knowing much about each other, both let their bodies speak, giving free rein to their lust. In this form of relationship, it is possible to fully demand and live out their desires and sexual fantasies. Value free! Both want the same. Quite an interesting experience that leads to new self-knowledge in the mutual understanding.

In contrast, there is the unique *"making love"* with the person for whom deep feelings - that is, pure love - are felt. This unique form of human closeness, coupled with sexuality, is dubbed by many as the absolute ectasias they crave and seek.

? Now ask yourself critically the questions of how your previous sexual experiences compare with your desire. How far are your experiences compared to your wishes? What do you want? What are you dreaming about? Make sure you do not judge yourself. It is your book, thoughts, cravings. It is not reprehensible to admit these to yourself.

_____

_____

119

What is your body longing for? What does he ask for?

_____

If you find it difficult to answer these questions in one go, please take your time. It may well be that your inner desires are not yet fully visible to you. You may have dropped a lot of dust over the years and now it takes time to remove this rubbish. Through your efforts to find answers, you have already initiated your thinking process. Make sure you always have something to write with, so you can write down lightning thoughts that will adjust. It is forming. The seeds are sown. The more answers you dig up and write down, the clearer your picture of what you really want.

What is your conclusion from these trains of thought, from this research journey? What do you learn from that?

_____

Summary Result

Sex... right at the first time?

When I was a teenager and my body was slowly becoming that of a woman, I heard several times from women in my family the famous saying, *"Do not give yourself up the first time ... You make yourself a lot more interesting if you fidget the man a little bit leaves..."*. Was this the same with you?

TIP

A wise saying that has a lot of truth in it, as I learned over the years. I admit that I did not always adhere to this saying (it would be only half the fun, right?). All the more I can personally confirm from my experience just how incredibly important it is that the man may pursue his hunting instinct. Yes, yes! It is for the man the ups and downs to woo, to surround and to strive for the sacrifice of his desire. Few men openly admit this. In most cases, they are not aware of their own behaviour, partly driven by their genes.

If you are really interested in a man, if you have already developed feelings for him and want more from him than just a one-night stand,

120

then clearly only one rule applies:

No sex the first time!

Why? Ladies, you make you more interesting, you wake up this desire after hunting in the man and you are clearly the target in his eyes. Try to put yourself in perspective for a moment. Would you enjoy it, if the game the hunter has been watching for weeks just lies down in front of him to surrender?! To stark comparison? But basically it is the same with you as a woman.

If the man struggles, leaning out the window, investing time and all his charm to conquer you as a woman, then you become more interesting as a woman for the man. Any man who instantly loses interest just because you do not immediately surrender to him at the first dates is not worth the thought. Believe me!

I even go so far as to say that if you are seriously interested in a man, you can use the strategy of "surrendering to yourself" or "stepping into the box" with you as long as we can.

That makes the voltage really electric and the adrenalin is really awakened.

Ladies, this is the absolute expression of your thoroughbred woman in you. With our sexual charms, we have a huge attraction for the men and these do not have to be handed over all at once, but in nibbles. You are the beautifully packaged package - beautiful with a gold bow - and this is now in front of him. How much do you think he smiles at this bow and pull away the wrapping pape...

It works wonders. As a thoroughbred woman, you carry this patience and this knowledge in you. Now it is also necessary to implement this. You make yourself more interesting with the man and are much more exciting, if he just does not get the whole package in one.

It is also a question of respect. Uniting your body with someone else's is a wonderful act as long as it is performed with respect and appreciation. This act becomes especially beautiful when, in addition to sympathy, respect and interest, deeper feelings such as love are added. By that I do not mean directly the Romeo and Juliet love, but the love in the form of a young seed that has the potential for something bigger.

To give time to this mutual growth and to increase the expectation with restraint in the sexual activity, results in a unique sensation, which is rewarded with an intensifying pleasure & increased tension.

I speak from experience. With this acting, with this decision "*to take it slow*", some men fell through my grid. I am grateful for that. Likewise, I experienced wonderful experiences that I would not have experienced in such a form and intensity with a quick one-night stand. My clear decision was: **I did not want to be one out of many!** I have always been too good for that. Because I know that as a full-blooded woman, I fully support my principles and decisions. Because that is one of the true strengths of a thoroughbred woman.

What do you take with you from these lines? Do you want to give your thoroughbred wife this space, time and freedom?

_____

_____

Menopause... and then?

Cycles are part of life. Indispensable facts of the earth. This reflects nature with the four seasons and keeps in the human body inexorably rest. This reflects the normal aging process, which is subordinate to all worldly creatures and life forms. This is nothing to shake and is not changeable.

The female body shows a special cycles development. After the monthly menstruation heralds the possibility of birth at the age of 15 years on average, the woman between the ages of 45 and 55 enters into a new form of being a woman. Admission to the menopause! For many women, the menopause is a dramatic experience. The fact that they no longer have the ability to give birth enables women to doubt their femininity. They no longer feel like women and retire in their new being instead of nourishing and growing in this new form.

Meanwhile, this entry into the menopause offers new prospects & opportunity. Used as a location determination, both family and professional, this experience offers the beginning of a new phase of life.

Being a woman does not mean having monthly bleeding. Nor does it mean being a thoroughbred woman if a woman can give birth to children. But on the contrary! Every single step, the process of being completely a woman, means coming closer to one's own authenticity and developing it.

This begins with the growth of one's own body, the onset of menstrual bleeding, experience of this femininity. This includes closing the circle of the cycle by ending the span of the bearing. Mother Nature closed the door to this miracle, but at the same time managed to open a new gate.

The intensity of one's own sexuality may well increase in sensitivity, since it no longer requires measures in terms of contraception. Of course, always mindful of a monogamy relationship. Indispensable in a polygamy or one-night stand-built relationships is the condom, as this protects against STDs and AIDS. In addition, more mature women have discovered a purer and respectful love for their body, which increases the intensity of sexuality.

Whatever form of relationship you live in, it is crucial that you accept, enjoy and live as a thoroughbred female. Especially from the beginning of the menopause!

Lust in harmony with life in balance

As a thoroughbred woman you know your lust and know how to deal with it. You talk to her, give her the attention, care for her, respect her and live her as well as it suits you.

If you still cannot fully relate your lust, then recognize that you as a thoroughbred woman are fully aware of it. Maybe a bit subliminal, but it is bubbling in you.

When we talk about the pillars of life, we usually talk about the 4 areas of meaning, occupation, partnership and body. In a broader sense, I see life in balance according to the 5 pillars of the identity of H.G. Petzold, which builds up as follows:

- **Job & Job:** What is my vocation?
- **Material Security:** How am I financially?
- **Value & Goals:** What are my values? My goals?
- **Body & Appearance:** What is really good within body?
- **Social contact:** Who do I want to spend time with?

Since these 5 parts are directly connected, the "lust for ..." is found in all areas as an indispensable, important factor that puts the spotlight in general in the limelight.

In this consideration arise many forms of pleasure. Such as cooking, in which the most intense fragrances animate the versatile taste senses and the intense desire to taste this treat that makes mouth-watering. Or the careful sniffing at an intense fragrant flower, which leads you with closed eyes on a flower meadow and you feel the great desire to rush with open arms into this endless colourful sea of flowers.

I experience the ritual of photographing as a comedy in which I capture the moment through the camera lens in hundredths of a second. Likewise, it is pure pleasure for me to listen to the different musical styles in a relaxed way, while exploring the different flavours of a red wine. When I feel my body in absolute flow during a kilometre-long run, an unbelievable feeling of pleasure makes me embrace the world. Each of these pleasure sensations is a feeling highlight!

As a thoroughbred woman, I use these conscious steps to nurture my lust desire and thereby increase. At the same time I let myself be removed from any barriers and obstacles of my pleasure sensations. On the contrary. I am and always remain experimental!

Be also experimental!

What do you do to inspire your desire to animate your desire? How do you train your pleasure sensation?

_____

_____

What will you integrate more consciously in your life in the future to perceive and enjoy more of your pleasure?

_____   **Summary Result**

_____

_____

The 5 main guiding principles, findings from this chapter are:

Make decisions, NOW

Every change begins with the first step of deciding. That is exactly where the hacking is. It is amazing how hard people make a decision. Irrelevant in which areas of life people are facing a situation or arrive at a crossroads. All have one thing in common: it is inevitable to choose a route.

Decision = Disconnect and let go

I have seen many people at work and in private who are struggling to make a decision themselves. Make your life enormously difficult by being pulled out into the extreme and at the same time being pushed away by cons. The tug-of-war of superlatives is introduced constantly.

What is left is fizzed energy and an even bigger question mark than before. In the fear remains in this questioning situation to make a wrong decision, then the path of passivity is chosen. Meanwhile, a wrong decision is always better than no decision to make. For life means to go, to move and not to remain or even to freeze.

As the word deciding already carries in itself, it is about the one thing: to divorce something, to separate. Release something to allow something new at the same time.

Where a door closes, a new one opens!

This is a valuable life wisdom! That sounds promising. We all want to experience something new, explore the unknown, get to know new things, explore new places.

Why is it so hard for us humans to let go of old?

For the most part, this builds on the fearful belief that the new is certainly not better than the old are. This behaviour shows what a basic attitude man has.

127

If he is daring, willing to take risks and has self-confidence, then he goes the new way. If he is anxious, despondent and quarrels with himself, he will remain in the old pattern, for he is rigid in thought and action. It comes to me the saying "*A bird in the hand is worth to in the bush*". In essence, it states that it is worth more to have a small benefit than the prospect of great benefit if it involves the risk of not having it in the end.

This behaviour is recognizable in many people. They lament their current situation, lament this continuously and pity themselves in their - in itself insoluble - malady. Instead, the solution, the new way, the new life is just One-step away.

The blinkers only allow the tunnel view along with the all proven way. It is important to take off the blinkers and change from the tunnel view into the vision! Who stands at an intersection has two options:

Option 1: Step back
The way back from where you came! This means not consciously engaging with the new, unknown, allowing all the opportunities, joys & experiences to pass un-lived. Instead, return to the old well-known.

Option 2: Look ahead of you
Taking the first step in the new direction. This means leaving behind the fear of the unknown and the unknown & instead paving the way for an unknown, exciting, new world. You know that everything will be fine and that your feminine instinct and intuition will guide you.

Which way you will go. One thing is clear:
You make a clear decision - in the here and now - a decision!

Whereby your decision in the NOW decides about your future in the morning. Your I AM tomorrow depends on your choices in the present. In other words, each of your decisions in the future will automatically have an impact on your future. Completely according to the law of cause and effect.

Thus, it is wise to make a decision. If you go back the way, nothing will change. You continue to stay in your hamster wheel and bravely continue pedalling. Meanwhile, your dissatisfaction will steadily increase and increase.

Do you consciously choose the way forward, you may enter uncharted realms, but these are full of adventure and arouse your spirit of discovery. Your curiosity, urge for research, joy for all that is new is pure joie de vivre (!), An elixir that leads you into new spheres of experience.

Practice

How is it with you? Are you standing at a crossroads? Do you have to decide? Do not you know any advice? The fear is plaguing you? In which situation are you?

_____

_____

What needs to be done? You know your answers. You know exactly where you should go. However, we tend to look for points of reference, that is, to seek affirmations that reinforce our aspirations.

Your intuition, your inner voice is yours a wise guide!

Give your attention to your intuition. Listen to yourself. What does your inner voice say? Listen carefully and you will find signs and answers. What did you learn from this? What do you decide now?

_____

_____

**Summary
Result**

Define your values

Values are qualities and qualities of life that we consider valuable and desirable. Every person carries values according to which he acts and aligns his life. In addition, we align our rules and principles

129

accordingly. Although these values give us fundamental orientation in life, we usually invest little or no time to become aware of them. So I invite you to become aware of your values.

Go in and write down all your values (such as luck and courage) that are important to you in your life. Ask yourself the following questions: What is important to you? What values do you live for? Are you determining? Do you value? At the end of the book you will find a list of values (page 169) that will help you in your selection.

_____

_____

_____

Now you have a good insight into your values to align your life. Now it is about defining your 5 most important values, because these are the ones that guide you the most. It is important for you and your life to know your values. In stages of decision, you let yourself be guided by these values, whether consciously or unconsciously.

How do you find out now your most important values?

1. Read your list with your value.

2. If values are listed in parallel, then remove one of them.
   (for example, freedom & independence are values that are similar)

3. Choose from 5 values that are extremely appealing to you.

4. Check if your selection comes deep from your heart.

5. Create a description of your 5 chosen values.
   (For me, freedom means ...)

6. Decide now!

130

Follow these steps and you will find the values that are important to you. Write down your 5 most important values:

1. _____

2. _____

3. _____

4. _____

5. _____

Knowing your values means knowing yourself.

A thoroughbred woman knows her values very well and follows them accordingly. Always check your values, because life likes to give us new values. Likewise, the valences shift.

What seemed important yesterday still is irrelevant today and completely unimportant tomorrow? Therefore, regular questioning is necessary, leading to a better understanding of your ego.

How did you experience this elaboration, the definition of your values? Did you find it difficult? What did you learn from it?

_____

Summary Result

Where is your journey going?
Knowing the destination of your journey is indispensable to achieving it. All of us have only been given a limited amount of time on this earth. Thus, there is no time to waste, to become aware of and strive for its goal.

What is your goal?
Many people do not know the answer to this question.
Hesitate and think. How is it with you? Do you know your
goal (s)? Wishes? Dreams? Keep this in writing and free of charge:

_____

You carry in you a compass, a radar device, which leads you
purposefully to your goal. Likewise, you are equipped with a
wonderful body - your body - that also supports you with its marvel
of power to guide you to your goal. Added to this is a perfect
software - your brain - that once your target has been entered into the
GPS, you will see the different routes. It is up to you to decide which
route to choose. With all these perfectly synchronized tools you have,
it is all about realization and targeting. However, these utensils do
not help you if you do not know where your journey is going.
Ich vergleiche dies mit einer Reise über das Meer.

> I compare this to a journey across the sea. As the captain of your
> ship - this may be a modern speedboat, a graceful three-masted
> sailboat or a pirate ship - you stand proudly on the bridge. The
> wind is blowing, the engine is roaring, the applied brake tugs and
> your crew looks at you expectantly and waits ... What? At your
command!
Exactly ... Everything is ready ... And yet it does not move forward.
Why? Your team still does not know where the journey is going.
They are waiting for your order, your destination. Now you have to
announce where the journey is going.

You are the thoroughbred woman who knows exactly what she
wants. She knows her inner reputation, knows her destination,
knows exactly what she is up to. She knows it is time to name it black
and white. Knows that the brakes have to be solved because the wind
is perfect, the weather is perfect and the timing is perfect. Confess…

Where is your journey going? Write without thinking - without judging - what your inner voice screams. What do you dream and dream about? Where should your ship take you?

_____

_____

_____

_____

Could you make your target clear ship?

As a thoroughbred woman, you carry all the answers in you! That is a fact! It is all about breaking your walls of doubt, fear, and insecurity. No one but yourself knows you are goals, your desires, your aspirations, even your vocation better.

TIP

If it does not slip at first with the answers, do not be too strict with yourself. It often takes time to wipe away the dust. Stay tuned. It is important that you deal with this topic from now on. Question yourself. Be vigilant and watch yourself in your environment. You will be presented with signs that present your answers.

What did you learn from this journey? What do you take with you?

Summary Result

_____

How far away are you from your destination?

After defining your goal, the question is how far you are from it. After all, it is about realizing it. That is why it is good to know where you stand and what it takes to get to your destination.

People believe that it is done by realizing, recognizing, establishing, naming the goals and a good dose of positive thinking. That is not correct!

133

That would be wonderful if it was that easy. However, more is needed. Every athlete will confirm this. But with wishful thinking and positive encouragement, his muscles do not grow. Daily hard exercising and continuous increase in weight make his muscles shape. This brings him daily closer to his goal of successfully running the marathon. Thus, this means for each of us:

Achieving goals means consistently working on them!

In this context, it is indispensable to make clarifications to find out what it takes to reach your goal. Do you want to become a successful entrepreneur? Then you have to acquire the necessary knowledge based on further education or study. A coach or mentor can also give you valuable tips along the way. Do you long to open a horse ranch on a Finca in Mallorca? Without the necessary language skills, such as Spanish, nothing works and the necessary management knowledge can be of tremendous benefit to you.

This means that recognizing your goal is only the beginning. Your initiative, action, putting into action decides whether you will successfully achieve the goal.

The motto is: ACT !
That is the main rule and you cannot shake it. There are no **TIP** excuses and no compromises. As the word compromises already stated, it is all about. Forgetting knowledge is a no-go.

Do you want to realize your goal? Do you want to walk the path with all the consequences and deprivations? Is the realization of your goal your deepest call? Do you want to combine all your strengths to reach your goal?

_____

_____

Yell your loudest YES. Because you will need tremendous strength, infinite energy, uninterrupted stamina, and the indomitable will to achieve your goal. You also need that burning in you, that deep heart's desire, that clear vision that makes you tingle your finger.

If you do not feel this deep desire, it can only mean one thing: you have not really defined your true goal, your inner call goal, your vocation, but filtered out a smaller milestone goal instead.

That means? You have to question yourself again and ask your inner voice for answers for you so crucial topic. If you are ready to race for your heart's purpose with waving flags in the finish area, it needs the following:

TIP

- Create a target board with pictures and spells of your target.

- Determine what it takes to achieve the goal.

- Create a clear Goal Achievement Plan (To-Do & Schedule).

- You stay consistent.

- Be ready to give up things.

- Do at least 3 things a day to get closer to your goal.

- Connect with your target/vision board several times a day and feel what it feels like to realize your goal.

- Record your goals every day in your lucky journal.

- Write down your achievements daily in your Lucky Journal.

**You are only one step away from your goal!
And the first!**

Once you have decided to reach your goal with all the consequences and milestones it takes to go in a consistent and unwavering manner, you are already on the target field! The only one who stands in the way of realizing your goals is only one person: YOU YOURSELF!

Get rid of your doubts, remove these heavy shackles and make your way determined. Your goal is already waiting for you! What is your conclusion from this? What knowledge and lesson have you learned?

_____

Do not doubt, instead act courageously

To doubt yourself and your cause costs a lot of energy and does not take you one-step further. On the contrary! Doubt promotes regression. *Doub-t* carries the word two/double in itself. It has two sides, two ways, two points of view, two choices to choose from. The question is, in which direction does your own doubt drag you? What do you ultimately choose?

"Doubt is the shadow of a man in the dark..." says a Japanese proverb. You as a full-blooded woman are not standing in the shade, but in the light, in the spot of your life. You know what you want, where your journey is going, where you can steer your ship and with all your strengths and abilities skilfully and with the best of your knowledge and conscience can be drawn across the sea. You always have your goal in mind.

The opposite of doubt is **faith, courage** and **trust**.

That you as the thoroughbred woman are the ultimate model for courage is beyond question. Maybe not for you, but for the rest of the world. You carry all confidence in you. Even as an embryo, you trusted that everything is good. That you come into the world alive and well. Perfect confidence in the tremendous energy and power of the universe lies within you. So too the knowledge of your own abilities and talents, which you have already used successfully several times. These are wonderful parameters for your own belief in yourself. You do not believe me?

Look for parameters, proofs that made you shine with your qualities: where were you brave? Where did you put your fear in the shadows and your courage?

136

_____

_____

ractice

Where did you let yourself be guided by your trust and trust in a new cause?

_____

**As a thoroughbred woman you carry
the legacy of Cleopatra in you!
You are powerful, energetic, creative, convincing with all your
wonderful outstanding and individual
Talents and skills.**

These has been given to you to follow your goals, your calling. There is no room for doubt. Fill it with courage, trust and faith in you. What are you taking with you?

_____

Summary
Result

Self-Confidence at the push of a button!
Knowing what is in you is crucial. In hours of doubt, of struggling, your self-confidence is the factor that decides to move on or stand still. If you are convinced of yourself, this urges you to go on, continue exploring, to elicit.

As a thoroughbred, you carry a tremendous amount of skills in you. In the run-up, we have identified your talents & strengths and called by name. Now name and note 5 of your most concise and talented talents that will boost and support your self-esteem.

1. _____

Practice

2. _____

3. _____

4. _____

5. _____

Do you recognize your genius that you carry in you? Everyone fills in your cell? Which makes you?

You are a source of power that nourishes your environment. Your laughter, your energy is a grief for those around you. You have a vocation, a goal that you will focus on achieving.

> You are a volcano of POWER and ENERGY.
> With these skills, you make the world a better one.

That means: You make positive changes. Exercise in the process of remembering your 5 most striking talents and strengths when in doubt. Because these will be your faithful and unwavering advisors and companions. Ask yourself the following questions:

1. Will my strengths and talents help me realize this?

_____

2. To what extent do my talents and strengths promote my implementation? What do I have to pay attention to?

_____

3. In addition to my strengths and talents, do I need any other help / support to meet my challenge of achieving goals?

_____

> As a thoroughbred woman, you skilfully put your talents & strengths to work and realize your goal.

> As a full-blooded woman, you keep your access to your self-confidence constantly open so you can always access it.

What do you take as a conclusion from it?

_____

What are you waiting for? Decide to go NOW!

Clearly: It is up to you. Your values, your goal, faith, your courage, trust and above all your strength and energy. It is said that it is time to go NOW. Not tomorrow, not the day after tomorrow or next week ... NOW!

Every change begins with the first step, which is a law of life that is unavoidable and unchangeable.

Make the decision - here and now - that as a thoroughbred you take your life, your helm and live your life the way you want it. Write down your decision now.

Every written word has much more effect than the thought, than the unspoken.

**Everything starts with the decision, your decision.
Stop complaining! Stop the hesitation!**

**From now on action, active implementation is announced,
are you clear ship have reached your goal.**

What decision do you make now? What is your decision? What will you do now? What is your goal? Which of your attributes support you? When do you start with it?

1. What decision do you make now? What is your decision?

_____

_____

139

2. What are your next steps?

_____

_____

3. What are your goal(s)?

_____

_____

4. Call your 5 most strengths with which you achieve your goals:

_____

_____

5. What does it take to realize your goal (s)?

_____

_____

6. What do you have to do?

_____

_____

7. What support will you require?

_____

_____

8. When do you start with it? When do you start?

_____

_____

Well then... Let's go for it!

The 5 main guiding principles, findings from this chapter are:

Your new ME & your environment

Any change in the environment causes surprise, incomprehension, amazement and lead to questions. *"Why are you doing this?" "Why are you changing this?" "Why do not you leave everything as it is?" "Everything was great. I do not understand why you want to change this now..."*

It is challenging for humans to ask critical questions while at the same time quarrelling with their own questions. Your decision to change - the first step in a new direction - is still very young, fragile, virginal and therefore extremely vulnerable. It is a young seed to be protected to withstand the pack of critical questions.

Surely, it will be easier for you to handle it when you realize how people basically handle change. Usually rather bad. This is normal. Why? Because there is a urge deep in people to be in their comfort zone and not to leave. In his comfort zone, he feels comfortable, knows his way around, and is well versed with the predictable developments. Changes are not included in it. Change means moving OUT of the comfort zone and entering a new, unknown world. That can be scary. This is true for any person who dares to step out of his comfort zone but also for the people and their partners, family and friends. What do I mean by comfort zone?

Get out of the comfort zone!
With comfort zone I mean the area in which the person feels comfortable, feels safe, and knows well. This refers to the zone in which man moves day in, day out. In his home, his circle of friends, in the execution of hobbies, in the workplace, in his well-known environment. Say, in all areas where a person is well versed, knows what to expect and he gets along well. This makes everything easy and there are no major hurdles, overcoming and efforts in this so-called comfort zone. Habits and everyday rituals are an elementary part of the comfort zone

However, the comfort zone ends where overcoming or effort begins & it is thus not so comfortable anymore. Everything new, unknown, strange & unexpected is outside the comfort zone. Fears are a very good indication that humans are leaving their comfort zone.

Everybody creates - mostly unconsciously - his own comfort zone. He develops an important zone for him, which he subconsciously defends as his sacred familiar zone. Likewise unconsciously, we quarrel with leaving that comfort zone so familiar to us. We notice this especially when we get into a situation in which a serious decision to leave the comfort zone leads us.

You actively worked through this workbook and decided to pursue your goal. You are moving on a new unknown path. Once you have decided to take the first step to change, you are also ready to leave your comfort zone.

Congratulations. Great ... I am proud of you!

Be proud of yourself, too! Take on that glorious feeling of new wind that now blows you after you step out of your comfort zone. That is wonderful. Pure sense of conquest that will flow through you. Take this feeling truly inside of you. Enjoy this and save it in your cells.

What is your conclusion from this?

Summary Result

_____

What may the neighbours say?
Your environment may not respond as positively to this change. You will be confused and not understand why you are seeking these changes. You will be confronted with critical questions that may unsettle you. For your family and friends, breaking out of your comfort zone is something they cannot understand. They do not understand it.

Be aware that there are only small fractions of people who seek to change themselves. These people will understand, support and promote you. While these people can understand your urge, most people cannot understand it. As well as? They themselves continue to move to their comfort zone and although they moan, they continue to run in circles in their familiar zone.

You expand your circle! You're ready to climb over hurdles and stones to leave your comfort zone, to learn new things, to experience and thereby expand yourself and your ME. By doing so, you automatically create a larger area where you will move from then on.

TIP

Thus, for you as a thoroughbred, it means being strong, consistent and staying true to your own determination. You can do that because you carry tremendous determination and courage in you. Remember, you are the heir of Cleopatra, who managed to win the then largest empire. In addition, you will be a role model for others with your behaviour and actions. Even if they will not immediately admit this, you will impress them with your behaviour, with your decision. Some will get the impulse to think about their own lives. Is not that a wonderful thought? You promote the life of others to a more positive turn with your actions. It takes some time, though.

Therefore do not concentrate on other people anymore! Instead, direct your thoughts and actions on you at the very beginning, since your decision is still fragile. Go your chosen path and do not engage in discussions with critical and negative people. Instead, explain to them kindly but determined that this is now your new path and you thank you in advance for their support. Point!

It is your life and your way.
No one else has the right to deny you that.
Always remember this!

!

Show me your friends and I will tell you who you are!
Not to be underestimated are the people with whom you surround yourself a lot. Our circle of friends has a significant influence on us as

we look at their behaviour. Quite imitating us in our environment. The phrase "*Show me your friends and I tell you who you are...*" is an ancient wisdom that carries a lot of truth in itself.

TIP

It is critical to question which friends we deal with and spend our time. Automatically colours the attitude, behaviour of your friends on you. Ask yourself: Who are your friends? How are they? Critical, sceptical, negative or cheerful, energetic, warm, positive people?

_____

_____

Friends are always our mirror. We reflect in them and can learn a lot from them. Especially in your turn, in the phase of change, friends are either obstructive or beneficial.

Be vigilant and mindful.
Do not let the critical words of yours get you out of your concept.

You have decided on it and are now marching purposefully and purposefully in your direction.

I have made various friendships over the course of my changes. I named the things by name and got us straight out of our comfort zone. This caused outrage and incomprehension in my counterparts.

Why did I do that?

I realized that some of my friends were traveling very negatively. They were caught in a maelstrom of whining, disappointment, resignation. Being sceptic, their focus was on negativity, distrust, and above all, fear. As a result, they did not want to leave the extreme need to leave their comfort zone - who knows what followed - with all their might. Although they were unhappy and dissatisfied. In addition, they criticized my actions, judged my decision as wrong, and continually converted me to insight. I recognized their concern for me in their actions; however, I reflected in their actions their own longing of breaking out. The result was an unfulfilled sense of resignation, as they did not make their way.

What happened?
I found myself in the position of justifying, explaining. At the same time, my own energy level dropped extremely, which I then lacked on my own - new - way.

One of my decisive steps in my change process was the decision that I wanted to have a circle of positive friends, humorous people who act purposefully and lived by similar values as I did. These friendships are not claims, expectations, but consistently nurturing and beneficial. That should not mean for you that you should now separate yourself from all your rather critical friends. With these words I want to give you food for thought and possibilities.

It is all in your hands and in your eye as well: **Look at your friends you are looking into your mirror.** Learn to understand yourself better through your circle of friends, to recognize and draw your conclusions from it.

What are your next steps? What do you decide in relation to your friends and acquaintances?

_____

Summary
Result

Do you have your compass by your side?
It makes sense, for the sake of your own self, to bring your compass into your field of vision, guiding you through the stream of extraneous and impassable detours. This compass reminds you where you are aiming. The danger that you lose sight of your goal is constantly present in everyday life.

So what to do? As a full-blooded woman, you have a firm will that drives you. Part of the game is your passion that gives you the absolute kick in your vision. This is your fuel that makes your engine run really well.

146

Nonetheless, you know that tools integrated into your everyday life are more than useful to give you back support. In doing so, you are laying the foundation from the very beginning to give yourself the best possible help to reach your destination safely and without much detour. You are yourself the best teacher and your own controller. That may seem like an exaggeration to some. However, as a thoroughbred woman, you are well aware of how fast the wind can turn and how you can get lost in the open sea and get lost.

Which tools will support you from now on?
The following tools will help you and serve you as a motivator, inspiration and reflection of yourself.

1. Happiness Journal

TIP 1

The magic of writing down is a force that will serve you wonderfully from now on. Especially in the daily use of a Happiness Journal you will experience sensational things that will show you much appreciation for yourself and will be an invaluable valuable compass for your goal orientation. What exactly is a lucky journal? It is a form of reflection book in which you daily write down your experiences of the day, reflect and revive your goal / vision.

This form of journal is a daily questioning with yourself. You are dealing with the answers to the questions:

- What are my goals?
- What am I grateful for?
- What are my achievements today? What did I do well?

You put things in the foreground, you hold them by the low writing, which you would forget unwritten again. Achievements are balm for the soul that you should remember. This will make your transmission smoother.

**To make another person happy,
makes you happy and envelops you with joy.**

Remembering your goals every day is important. You check your compass every evening, so to speak, if it points in the right direction. Through your consistent daily writing down, you automatically check the alignment of your goal every day. As a result, small deviations are faster noticeable and recoverable. As you lose sight of your target for several days or weeks, larger deviations are possible.

Start now with your lucky journal! A tool that does not take more than 15 minutes to fill out daily. Well invested 15 minutes deciding your future. At the end of the book you will find a template of the Happiness Journal page.

TIP 2

2. Goal & Vision Board

Take an A3 or A2 paper sheet & find pictures from the internet that you associate with your vision and goal. Do this spontaneously, without thinking twice. You can also use photos from a magazine. Cut out those pictures or headlines that appeal to you & paste them onto your so-called Vision Board/Vision Sheet.

Decorate it, as you like; stick things on it, banknotes or photos of your family. The important thing is that your board represents your goals and that you can completely identify with them when you look at them. The more spontaneous this happens, the more authentic it will become. It is best to give yourself a 15-minute timeline to create.

Then you stick your vision board on a wall. Every morning and evening, you connect to your board by placing your right hand on the paper, closing your eyes and imagining how you have already realized your vision, goals. Feel that joy, happiness that you perceive and anchor that sensation in your cells.

The more often you do this, the more intensively you will feel the realization of your goals and come one-step closer every day.

---

3. Cards / Post-It

I have been working for years with A5 format or post-it cards, which I use to write down my motivational sentences, messages, and reminders. Afterwards I place them in my apartment, in the car and on my worktable. There are places such as the bathroom mirror, front door (apartment interior side) as great place donors for these inspirational notes as well as on the laptop lid and the wardrobe. These written messages remind me of my goals during the daytime phases. Depending on the situation, when I see them I immediately have them on my screen and they are present to me.

---

4. Room of silence

That meditating is healing for our body-mind-soul is well known. For years, I tried meditating without success. The room of silence finally worked. How does this work?

Sit on the floor or chair. Close your eyes and imagine how you move away from your current location and approach a house. You open the door, enter the room and close the door. The room in full light is empty and silent! Take up this emptiness and silence and nourish yourself by the warming light.

Relax. Listen to your breath. Add a mantra by saying the words in your mind: "*I am in the here & now. I'm there. I'm ME. Thank you…*"

Try it yourself. If it does not work the first time, do not despair, but try again the next day. Start with one minute (*set the alarm clock on your smartphone*). Afterwards you increase to 2 for 5, 10 & 15 minutes.

To experience the *Nothing* in this form is an incredible experience! It nourishes energy, strength and cleanses. In addition, thoughts, ideas and insights come naturally to light. For me, entering the room of silence is the contact with my subconscious mind. The verbal communication with sub consciousness is an extraordinary way to get in touch with yourself.

It is worthwhile that you visit the room of silence in you! The more often you do that, the more intense and impressive your experience will be with it.

TIP
5

5. Tête-a-Tête Time

Reserve your personal time each day for you. I call this *"Tête-a-Tête Time"*. The best way to plan this time for you fix in your everyday life. Maybe early in the morning, when everyone is still sleeping. In this time, you are only dealing with you. Write in your lucky journal or enter the room of silence. Half an hour to one hour is ideal.

As a thoroughbred woman you use these aids. Now make the decision to integrate the mentioned tips into your everyday life.

Summary
Result

Open and transparent communication

Obviously, your daily routine, your routine, will change as you continue to pursue your goals (be it implementing tools, etc.). This not only affects yourself, but also your environment, your family and friends. As we have already mentioned, it may well be that your environment feels pushed by your changes in the head.

!

To avoid abuses in the first place, it is extremely useful to seek open, transparent communication by explaining to your important person how important these changes are to you. Especially what your goal is with it. You take the wind out of the sails in advance.

That does not mean that they fully support your intention, but you express with your open and honest attitude how ready you are for this path. First, state how important this new way is for you. Emphasize that you very much hope for the support, understanding and acceptance of family and friends and that it is important for you to know them behind you.

With open communication, you will get people into your boat, make them your accomplices, and pick them up with your élan.

If important people do not respond positively to your change, try not to take it personally. Give them time to digest. You show them with your consistent attitude that you as a full-blooded woman are 100% on your decision. That will impress your environment. Even if they will not tell you personally. Be aware that your determination is a virtue that will be admired.

Decide now: With whom will you speak when?

Summary
Result

What to do in case of stumbling blocks?

... stay cool and jump over it! That's too easy? That's what you should do. Galant jump over it. The more often you practice this, the easier it will be for you. No matter in what form incidents try to stand between you and your goal, stay focused!

Do not be discouraged by these hurdles
but come out of it stronger.

Obstacles make you an acrobat. You become a specialist in a tightrope act, gaining manoeuvrability and discipline. Your balance is trained and at the same time, you learn that nothing bothers you so quickly, out of your rest. *"If you are easily distracted, you have to take many detours,"* says a proverb. How true! As well as: *"All difficulties and obstacles are steps on which we rise in the air."*

The higher you go,
the more view you get of your goal, your vision!

Be an example for others...

Surely you have a role model. What exactly do you like about this person? What has this person done that makes him your role model? Write down your main impressions:

_____

You have talents and abilities in you that strive to be in the limelight. You are looking at a wealth of valuable experiences that you have gained on your hike. The coming miles will continue to shape you, strengthen you in your size. Your skills and talents, who were born to you as a thoroughbred woman, will support you:

- With the power of a lioness,
- with the mindfulness of a lynx,
- with the diligence of an ant,
- with the memory of an elephant,
- with the liveliness of a bee,
- with the cunning of a vixen,
- with the suppleness of a cat,
- with the grace of a swan,
- with the peace-making of the pigeon and
- with the strength of a tigress.

All these abilities you carry in you, are deep in your cells. Let them free and feel the enormous power, the irrepressible élan and clear call for the outbreak of all these phenomena.

Carry out this call to the outside, motivates people, especially women to follow their inner voice. To shed her shackles, to make her way with pride. Every human, every woman deserves it! You as a thoroughbred woman now know about this fact!

Inspire others,
by acting as an example
strive your way undeterred and
your gratitude will let you into the home stretch.

The 5 main guiding principles, findings from this chapter are:

Show gratitude

To practice gratitude is a virtue and is considered an indispensable attitude and action in many religions and teachings. To be aware of what is present is essential to the clear consciousness of consciousness. Specials for your own happiness.

Gratitude is a declaration of love to life

In our western society, great importance and importance are attached to material goods. The more expensive and the newer the better. The entire economic and marketing mechanism is geared to this and dominates us every day.

It does not matter what man possesses in goods, but what qualities and values he carries in himself. What valuable thoughts and actions he realizes and what man does for the benefit of others. The mere fact of having a perfect perfectly functioning body is a gift and the true value for which we should be extremely grateful.

As you already know, you are effectively influencing your perceptions by listing your personal appreciation for gratitude every day in your lucky journal. You become more alert, more balanced, calmer, and happier. You realize that it is just the little things that ultimately make the powerful feeling of bliss.

Thus, the wonderful claim that gratitude is a declaration of love to life is quite right.

That is the point. To question each day in the evening, for which you are grateful, is clearly a clear open view of your past day, including its encounters and experiences. This results in your decision as to what was good and appreciative that day, in other words, what you are grateful for.

If man simply lets the day rest within himself without subjecting him to reflection, it means at the same time that the chances of knowing pass by. You, on the other hand, clearly place your awareness and time in the direction of seeing, knowing and appreciating, which then leads to gratitude.

I recommend the following mindfulness exercise that you can do during the day. You take a handful of smaller stones or marbles that you put in your pocket. Every time you experience something beautiful during the day, take a stone from your right pocket and put it in your left pocket. If you do this vigilantly and continuously, at the end of the day, you have pushed numerous stones to the other side of the bag. In the **TIP** evening, when you empty your pockets, you remember each joyful experience that made the stone roll - in the truest sense of the word.

These experiences are added to your gratitude list, which are then part of your lucky journal.

Often I am asked the question, which experiences I mean by that. Now that can be completely different individually. Crucially, these actions have given you a beautiful and enriching feeling.

These can be quite unspectacular experiences, such as keeping the door open by an unknown person, the warm welcome of the cashier in the shop or the outspoken compliment of a colleague on your new dress. All these beautiful events enrich your day.

**Just the perception & recognition
the little things in life,
makes you a happy person.**

For example, what did you experience today that is great and beautiful? What gave you a great feeling? Who put a smile on your face today? Write down your experiences for which you are grateful.

_____

_____

_____

Did you find it difficult to remember your positive experiences? You will see, the more times you do that, the easier it will be for you.

Now make the decision that you will be more alert and attentive. You also write daily your positive experiences that fill you with gratitude.

Summary Result

_____

_____

For the benefit of all people...

Everything starts with the first step. As a thoroughbred woman, you have great power, outstanding abilities, and the focused gaze of an eagle. Use these talents and gifts wisely for the benefit of all.

To act for the benefit of all people is the highest law of life, which is supported by gratitude, esteem and love.

As the ego takes care of and pushes for one's own benefit, gratitude is expressed in the effort to do things that benefit the well-being of all. It is crucial which of the parties gains the upper hand. To work for the good of all sets a cycle in motion, which is reflected in our environment and us.

Sharing is an essential expression of what man has enough and he likes to give generously. This very clearly shows the law of attraction.

What you give (*with donations or good deeds*),
Will make your life rich (*with gifts*)!

Surrendering one-tenth of income for the benefit of others is one of the thoughts held in the Old Testament. If it is not financially possible for you to donate, then look for another way to help.

How about giving up your time by helping out in a social setting? Single pensioners visit the retirement home, dogs from the shelter go for a walk, etc.

Make every effort to think about what you can do for the benefit of others every month. I actively share and donate for years and I do so with great joy and conviction. It makes you grateful, humble and happy.

Look around you and see what you can contribute. Write down what comes to mind:

Practice

_____

_____

As a full-blooded woman, you are aware of your knowledge, of your responsibilities, use them fairly, wisely & in an effort to do the best for people, animals and nature. With your thinking, acting & acting you are aware of the law of cause and effect and know the effects.

What happens if you do this? As a thoroughbred woman - who is indispensable and continuously strives for the well-being of all - you will experience wonderful things, as you act in the wake of the laws of life as a motivator, as an inspirer and as a source of action.

How wonderful is that? What is your knowledge, your conclusion, your summary of it?

_____

_____

_____

_____

_____

Finally, I want you to follow
give valuable advice on your way,
that will change your life:

TIP

Live the life you want!

Join now and live as the
thoroughbred woman you are!

Believe in you!

You are a thoroughbred woman!
Thoroughly!

Perfectly powerful, energetic, feminine, sexy...

You are fantastic!

The 5 main guiding principles, findings from this chapter are:

Final word

Now we have arrived at the end of this book. At the same time, this is the beginning of your new life. Your new life, your being a woman, by turning the thoroughbred woman inside out, giving her air, space and energy, breathing her life into her limbs.

There is so much power and energy in you!
Get your thoroughbred woman out of the corner and let her breathe, act and above all, let her be active!

The thoroughbred woman in you is courageous, visionary and mindful in dealing with people and the environment. She knows your wishes and needs, and most of all, she knows about your talents and talents. Use this wisely as well as wise and you are heading for your dream life. You will experience so much great and new that you cannot even imagine now.

Believe in yourself, in your abilities and in your talents. I believe in you! Why?

Because women are
the pillars of society,
the powerhouse of families,
the peacemakers of the people,
motivators of the children and
the visionaries of the future.

Everything starts with the first step!
Take yourself by the hand and lead yourself into the light.
You are wonderful, energetic, wise, visionary & authentic!

You are a thoroughbred woman through and through!
Be grateful and...
live truly the thoroughbred woman you were born as!

ENJOY IT!

Notes

Notes

Notes

Attachments

Here you will find information that will help you in your personality development. On my homepage *www.creativita.cc* you can download some of this information.

Typical negative beliefs

We people carry around many negative beliefs that are very bothersome. Here is a small excerpt. (*source: www.zeitzuleben.de*)

- No pain no gain
- Love is blind.
- I am incapable/unimportant/ cowardly.
- I am not good enough.
- Nobody takes me seriously.
- Rich people are bad.
- The world is unfair.
- Everyone thinks only of himself.
- Money spoils the character
- I cannot say no.
- Life is hard.
- Money is dirty.
- All that glitters is not gold
- I am too shy.
- I am too stupid / awkward.
- I have to be modest.
- I have to keep order.
- I am unable to relate.
- Real men do not cry.
- I cannot show any weakness.
- I always have to be perfect
- The last will be bitten by the dogs.
- I must not disappoint others.
- My opinion is not interested.
- I do not have enough time.
- I cannot afford that.
- I am to unimportant.

- I do not deserve it.
- I cannot change.
- Schuster, stay with your last.
- I have to work.
- I am not good enough.
- There is nothing in vain in life.
- My parents / others are to blame.
- I have no talents.
- I have two left hands / feet.
- I am not capable of it.
- Others are better than me.
- He who shows feelings is weak.
- I do not deserve it.
- I have nothing to say.
- I am too inexperienced.
- I am too young / too old.
- I cannot change that.
- I am powerless.
- Success makes lonely.
- I am not worth it.
- I do not deserve this.
- I cannot do anything good.
- Others are better than me.
- I am just out of luck.
- I deserve no recognition.
- Nobody loves Me
- Everyone is against me.

Positive beliefs about personality development

With pleasure, I present you here my TOP 30 positive beliefs.

1. Everything I do will be a success.
2. Unlimited energy flows through my body.
3. I am an oasis of peace, love and joy.
4. I am the expression of perfect freedom.
5. I feel my body, mind and soul as a harmonious whole.
6. Unique & creative skills and talents flow through me.
7. I hear and trust my inner voice.
8. Intelligence, courage and self-esteem are part of me.
9. I can do everything I want to achieve.
10. I am a powerhouse of skills and talents.
11. My self-esteem and self-esteem are limitless.
12. I am calm, relaxed and satisfied.
13. I love myself very much.
14. I am worth loving.
15. I am under the protection of divine love.
16. I feel and enjoy my infinite vitality.
17. Every day I give and receive love again and again.
18. I am very valuable.
19. I trust my fellow human beings and they trust me.
20. I am a magnet of good.
21. I attract positive people with my positive power.
22. Life thrills me and fills me with new energy.
23. I feel my body as a harmonious whole
24. Each breath fills me with powerful energy.
25. My body is beautiful and supple.
26. I am a sparkling life.
27. Healing energy flows through my body.
28. I send out radiant power and put on everything that supports me.
29. My inner wisdom leads me and gives me a great life.
30. I am an expression of perfect freedom.

I recommend that you read, write and listen to these positive beliefs twice a day within the next 30 - 90 days. Take these on your smartphone. Have lots of fun with it!

Negative beliefs for wealth, prosperity and money

Here is a list of negative beliefs about money, prosperity and wealth.

- Money only worries.
- Money is not important.
- Money makes snooty and arrogant.
- Money is dirty.
- Money cannot buy happiness.
- Money is the root of all-evil.
- Money is not everything.
- There are more important things than money.
- All that glitters is not gold.
- Money spoils the character.
- I never have enough money.
- You do not talk about money.
- Money makes the world go round.
- Money stinks.
- Money makes you comfortable.
- Money runs through my fingers.
- Much money creates worries and problems.
- He who has a lot of money has many worries.
- Time is money.
- He who is rich has no true friends.
- When I am rich, I'm only loved because of my money.
- Money is hard to come by.
- Money does not grow on the trees.
- Rich people have been lucky and exploited others.
- Money makes you lonely.

Money alone does not make you happy

- I never get the big money
- You can only get a lot of money through ruthlessness and harshness.

Positive beliefs about wealth, prosperity and money

Gladly I present you here my TOP 30 positive beliefs for money, prosperity and wealth:

1. Money is positive energy.
2. I easily magically attract great wealth and money.
3. I love money. Money flows into my life.
4. I feel well with money.
5. I am infinitely rich and successful.
6. I feel fantastic with money.
7. I am attracting financial abundance.
8. I am happy and satisfied.
9. Money is my faithful friend and companion.
10. I am a money magnet and constantly attracting money.
11. Money is good for me.
12. Money flows effortlessly from multiple sources into my life.
13. I naturally attract money.
14. The money is on the street, I just have to get it.
15. I always discover new ways to make money.
16. I allow myself to own money.
17. I love to earn money and have fun doing it.
18. Money is an integral part of my life.
19. Money has a positive impact on my life.
20. I live my life in wealth and prosperity.
21. I have all conceivable financial possibilities.
22. I am at peace with money.
23. Money is good for me.
24. Money gives me the opportunity to do things that I want to do.
25. My money allows me a life of prosperity, abundance & abundance
26. I am worth asking for money.
27. Money does a lot of good.
28. Wealth is a natural state in my life.
29. I was given all the tools to obtain wealth.
30. Prosperity and abundance in all areas flow to me now.

I recommend that you read, write and listen to these positive beliefs twice a day for the next 30 - 90 days. Take these on your smartphone. Have lots of fun with it! *(source: www.affirmotionen.de)*

Overview of values

Here is a list of values that are generally considered desirable and ethically sound specifics. *(source: www.wertesysteme.de)*

acceptance
activity
adventure
aesthetics
affection
alertness
ambition
aim

attention
authenticity

bravery

care
calm
charisma
cheerfulness
courtesy
creativity
confidence
control
concern
conscientiousness
compassion
courage

decency
dedication
determination
discipline

enjoyment

economical
enthusiasm
engagement
ease
efficiency
empathy

Fairness
farsightedness
Friendship
Freedom
fun

gratitude
gentleness
generosity
gracefulness

harmony
health
humour
humility
honesty

idealism
imagination
innovation
integrity
intelligence
interest
intuition
independence
incorruptibility

justice
joy

loyalty
life quality

modesty
motivation

neutrality

progress
peace
patience

quality

openness
optimism

passion
persistence
punctuality
presence
process
prosperity

respect
realism
responsibility
reliability
recognition
receptiveness

reliability

sense of order
strength
self-discipline
self-confidence
sensitivity
success
safety
solidarity
Stability sympathy
serenity

thoughtfulness
trust
tradition
topicality
team spirit
tolerance
transparency

wisdom

My Happiness Journal   Date:_____

My Goals:

1. _____

2. _____

3. _____

What am I grateful for? _____

_____

_____

What did I do well today? What was successful for me?

_____

_____

_____

What did I do today to get closer to my goals?

_____

_____

Who am I happy with today?

_____

What am I proud of?

_____

Sex organ men and women

The great miracle of nature reflects in the marvel of the human body and its immense functions.

The human species is designed so that reproduction is assured.

A sophisticated, perfectly arranged system that is second to none. See the sex organs of the man and the woman - although different nevertheless perfectly matched.

(https://www.medicaldaily.com/male-and-female-reproductive-systems-harder-label-some-others-271039)

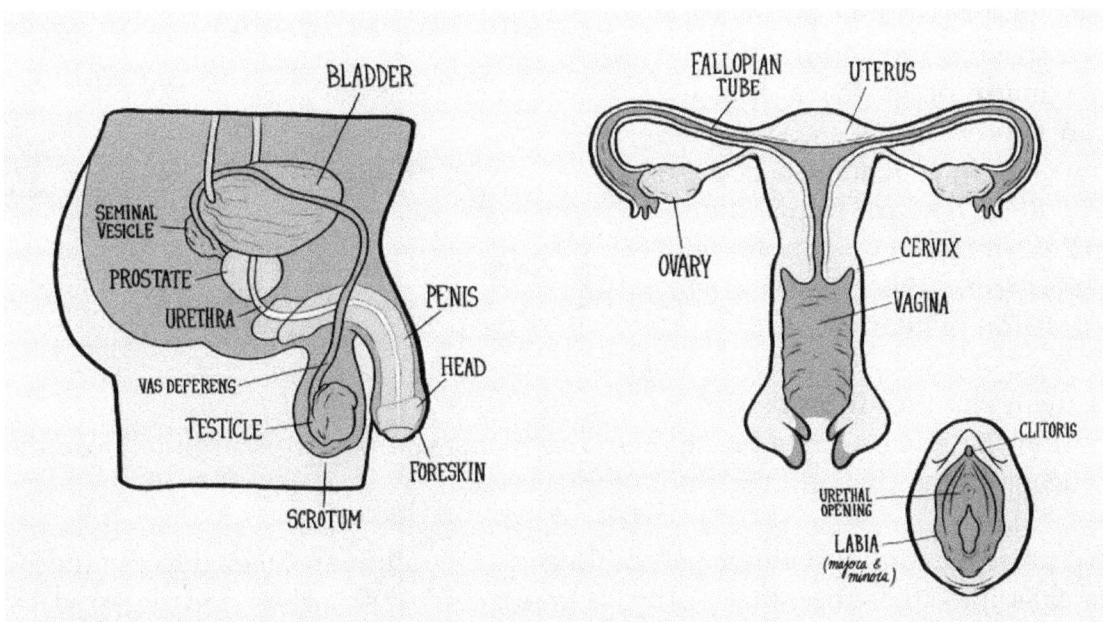

For all those women who would like to know more about themselves, their bodies and their sexuality, I can recommend the following homepage *www.womenshealthnetwork.com*. This good explanatory website is very specific and explanatory in the topic of sexuality for women and deals with the topic of masturbation. Have fun while reading…

Explanation of menstrual cycle

The cycle lasts about 28 days and begins on the first day of the menstrual period. 50% of all women experience a cycle between 23 and 35 days. Bleeding lasts for 3 to 7 days in most women. The woman loses about 60 ml of blood.

Over the course of a month, the uterus prepares for possible fertilization. The mucosa on the inner wall of the uterus grows so that a fertilized egg can nest in it. The fertile days are an average of 2 - 4 days during ovulation (see graph). While an ovum can survive and fertilize for a maximum of 24 hours, sperm can survive between 3 and 5 days (!) In a woman's body. The ideal time for fertilization is 2 days before ovulation and ends on the day after ovulation (ovulation).

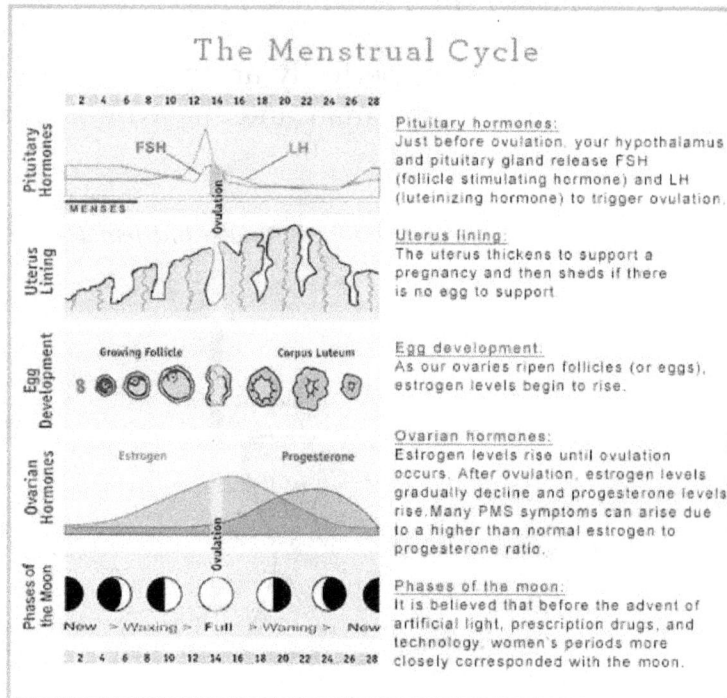

The Menstrual Cycle

Pituitary hormones:
Just before ovulation, your hypothalamus and pituitary gland release FSH (follicle stimulating hormone) and LH (luteinizing hormone) to trigger ovulation.

Uterus lining:
The uterus thickens to support a pregnancy and then sheds if there is no egg to support.

Egg development:
As our ovaries ripen follicles (or eggs), estrogen levels begin to rise.

Ovarian hormones:
Estrogen levels rise until ovulation occurs. After ovulation, estrogen levels gradually decline and progesterone levels rise. Many PMS symptoms can arise due to a higher than normal estrogen to progesterone ratio.

Phases of the moon:
It is believed that before the advent of artificial light, prescription drugs, and technology, women's periods more closely corresponded with the moon.

If there is no fertilization, this part of the mucous membrane dies. The menstrual period is used to rinse the mucous membrane remnants out of the body.

An unfertilized ovum either passes through the fallopian tubes into the uterus or falls into the abdominal cavity. It enters and is absorbed and digested by cells of the immune system.

While some women can hardly walk to work in pain during their days, others feel the desire for sex. According to a study carried out by Kinsey-Institute, 48% of women avoid genital sex during their period. Meanwhile, 15% of women surveyed said they had intercourse during their days. *(Source: www.womenshealtnetwork.com)*

You can find more valuable information on this topic on the homepage: *www.womenshealthnetwork.com*

172

Book Tips:

To increase knowledge means to readdaily! Selected nourishing works are helpful in this respect. I can recommendthe following books:

- *The Power of the Subconscious* of Joseph Murphy
- *The Secret* by Rhonda Byrne
- *The Wisdom of Buddhism; Day by Day* by Danielle Föllmi
- *Mars liebt Venus. Venus liebt Mars* by John Gray
- *The Alchimist* by Paulo Coelho
- *The richest man of Babylon* by G.S. Clason & A. Gittinger
- *A dog named Money* by Bodo Schäfer

Movie Tips:

- *Embrace, you are beautiful* - Documentary about slimming paranoia
  A remarkable film/documentary a must for all women!

- *The Shift - The Secret of Inspiration* by Dr. Wayne Dyer
  In this film about the ego, peopleexperience a quantum leap and thereb ychange their view of the world and theirlives.

Recommended Links:

- *www.womenshealtnethwork.com*
  Great explanation side, which goes very specifically andexplainingly int o the topic Sexuality forwomen. I can only recommend it to anywoman who wants to know more aboutherself, her body and her sexuality.

- *www.zeitzuleben.de*
  Acomprehensive online guide tomindfulness, success, communication, life planning and motivation.

Vita by Carmen C. Haselwanter

Born on June 24, 1969, the author grew up in a family of two thousand at the Inn in the heart of Tyrol in the company of caring parents and two brothers.

As an open-minded, inquisitive child, she watched the world from an early age with watchful, curious eyes. As a book rat, she read everything she could get her hands on. Even at an early age, she felt the urge to travel the world. While schoolmates chose to study or teach, as a teenager, they decided to accept life as the true study.

Carmen C. Haselwanter was fortunate to have open-minded, modern parents who supported her dream. After successfully completing a 2-year private school and then gaining her first professional experience as a credit assessor in a mail-order company, she was on the plane to London at the age of 17! A minor who made his way to the British capital was an unusual undertaking for the small hometown, which was quite surprising.

For Carmen C. Haselwanter, this step out of her comfort zone started a world full of adventure, excitement and challenges. In the metropolis of London, where she initially worked as an au pair, she recognized the endless opportunities offered by this multi-cultural metropolis. She grabbed this full of energy! Because of her extraverted, approachable nature, she quickly became friends with people from all over the world. She was fascinated by the enormous diversity that distinguished people - and especially women - from different cultures. When she worked as an assistant in a Jewish nursing home, she listened with deep emotion to the dramatic narratives of German and Austrian refugees from the Second World War. Serving a Jewish diamond grinder in the heart of London, she came to know and appreciate the Jewish business sense.

After 1 ½ years, the 18-year-old left the British capital and moved on to explore the world. It should cities such as Amsterdam, Paris, Athens and Zurich as well as countries such as Italy, France and Switzerland are temporarily their home, where they developed their professionally

174

creative. She sold self-created fashion jewellery on markets, acted as a street music artist, worked as a fair host and tourist guide in major European cities. At that time, she realized how easy her access to the people fell. During this intense time, her desire to write, which she had nurtured since childhood, developed into an indispensable process that helped her to process the multitude of impressions.

Fascinated by the metier hotel subject, the Tyrolean worked various winter seasons in Austria and Switzerland. Initially as a room-maid and later as a receptionist and management assistant. Her good knowledge of foreign languages proved to be of great benefit.

Her desire to travel and discover new cultures led her at the age of 24 to an 8-month tram trip through Central America. An impressive journey that revealed the uncomplicated, hearty nature of Latin Americans with their passionate music. Intrigued by this, she found herself on a cruise ship belonging to the shipping company *Costa Crociere*, where she sailed as captain secretary in officer status through the Caribbean Sea. At that time, women accounted for almost 10% of the total crew of 500 people. This unusual working and living environment should prove to Carmen C. Haselwanter extremely instructive and interesting.

After her return from this floating world, she began to work for the Austrian tour operator *Touropa* as a tour guide. A perfect combination, combining her passion for travel with the profession. Carmen C. Haselwanter loved this wild time of traveling. The variety and challenge of finding a solution with previously unknown problems was pure adrenaline for her. After working in the Canary Islands, Balearics and Greece, she found herself station manager on a Greek island. She felt a deep bond and sympathy with the land of the gods, the home of mythology and the hospitable people.

In the middle season she completed courses in graphic design & computer programming. After her desire to express her love of creativity became more intense, she went to the 7 million city of Athens. A little later Carmen found himself sending out over 250 applications (*at that time still all printed and sent by post*) in a small advertising graphics company, where she worked as a web designer creative work. In addition, she acted as project manager for new customer acquisition from German-speaking countries.

Knowing that every end is a fresh start, she was looking for new opportunities after she left the land of mythology in 2002. At the age of 33, the globetrotter saw a lot of life, work experience, and felt the need to use her expertise in a new field. When she was offered employment as a management assistant in the newly opened Casino St. Moritz, she did not hesitate for long.

With inexhaustible zest for action, she entered a new world full of contrasts! St. Moritz, known internationally as the Top of the World for luxury and glamor, as well as the world of casinos, which had to gain a foothold in Switzerland as a new industry.

The author actively took advantage of this time by attending courses, colleges and a university, where she graduated in 2012 with a master's degree in advanced studies (MAS). As a dissertation, she dealt with the topic "*Creativity, the key resource of the present and the future for small businesses*". She trained as a coach and her apprenticeship as a spiritual coach should serve as the perfect entry point for the Business & Systemic Coach. Meanwhile Carmen climbed up the corporate ladder in Europe's highest casino, after having been entrusted to each other the positions of Administration Manager, Human Resources and the responsibility of the Marketing Manager.

During this time, she discovers another of her passion: event management, where she lets her creativity run wild. At the same time, she founded the company "*Creativitá*", in which she incorporates creativity management in the areas of living, writing, photos and coaching.

Everyone is creative for the creative manager. The difference lies in the recognition and the individual benefit. She says: "*We all have a deep creativity in us. But not everyone leaves their room.*"

After assuming the function of Deputy Director for 1 ½ years, Carmen C. Haselwanter took over the management of Casino St.Moritz as Director in July 2014 and became the second female director of the Casinos Austria International Group. For 4 years, the Austrian has been working in this position and finds this activity exciting every day, as direct contact with people gives her a lot of fun, joy and inspiration.

An elementary part of the artist's life is to live out her own creativity. She does this by expressing her passion as a photographer, artist (using wood as her favourite material), author and blogger.

The fact that the sum of their experiences in books now finds access to people fills them with pride! *"I am immensely grateful that my life is filled with so much diversity, opportunities and happiness. It is a deep need for me to encourage people - especially women - with my words and experiences. I want to show you that every human being can reach for the stars. It is crucial to make the decision and go at least one-step in this direction every day!"*

According to Carmen's motto: *"Everything is possible, as long as humans overcome their own walls!"*

Information

You want to know more about the author Carmen C. Haselwanter?
Visit her homepage and social media channels.

Instagram: www.instagram.com/carmencreativita/

Facebook: www.facebook.com/Kreativitaetsmanagement/
            www.facebook.com/carmen.haselwanter

Homepage:www.carmenchaselwanter.com
            www.creativita.productions
            www.PowerCoachOfTheAlps.com

You are also welcome to write an email to the author. Please use following address for this: info@creativita.cc

Other works

From the author Carmen C. Haselwanter who is working as a coach, photographer, project manager, creative manager, artist, entrepreneur and managing director, following publications have been published:

Lust... for Mr. Right?
ISBN: 978-3-907151-21-1

Lust... for Success? From Au-Pair to Casino Director in St. Moritz
ISBN: 978-3-907151-22-8

Come, I'll show you how beautiful Engadin St.Moritz is... in Autumn
Komm' ich zeige dir, wie schön Engadin & St. Moritz ist...
ISBN: 978-3-907151-00-6

Come, I'll show you how beautiful Engadin St.Moritz is... in Summer
Komm' ich zeige dir, wie schön Engadin & St. Moritz ist...
ISBN: 978-3-907151-05-1

Donation

By purchasing this book, you have not only done something good for yourself and/or made someone else happy with it, but you also donated at the same time. Yes, you did! How?

10% of the purchase price of this book goes to charitable institutions! The author is donating for years to charitable institutions such as Médecins sans Frontières, WWF, Greenpeace and numerous smaller organizations. Likewise, Carmen C. Haselwanter supports girls with a sponsorship in countries like Bali, Tibet / India etc.

THANK YOU FOR YOUR SUPPORT!

Live every day
as if you have been your whole life
just lived for this one day...